Capturing the Moon

Classic and Modern Jewish Tales

Retold by
Rabbi Edward M. Feinstein

BEHRMAN HOUSE INC
www.behrmanhouse.com

Project Editor: Alys Yablon Wylen
Book and Jacket Design: Masters Group Design, Inc. • Philadelphia

Copyright © 2008 by Edward M. Feinstein

Published by Behrman House, Inc.
11 Edison Place
Springfield, NJ 07081
www.behrmanhouse.com

Library of Congress Cataloging-in-Publication Data

Feinstein, Edward, 1954-
  Capturing the moon : classic and modern Jewish tales / retold by
Edward M. Feinstein.
     p. cm.
  Includes index.
  ISBN 978-0-87441-840-8
  1. Jews—Folklore. 2. Legends, Jewish. 3. Tales. I. Title.

  GR98.F45 2008
  398.208992'4—dc22

                              2008000966

Manufactured in the United States of America

★

This book is dedicated to my children,
Yonah, Nessa, and Raffi, who sat on my lap
and taught me how to tell stories
to the Children of Israel.

Contents

Acknowledgments

Astoryteller needs a listener. I am grateful to all the children and adults who have listened to my stories these many years: the children and families of the Levine Academy (formerly the Solomon Schechter Academy) of Dallas, Congregation Shearith Israel in Dallas, Camp Ramah in California, Valley Beth Shalom in Encino, California, and the Ziegler School of Rabbinic Studies at the American Jewish University in Los Angeles. I am grateful as well to all the communities that have so warmly welcomed me and my stories.

I am grateful to Alys Yablon Wylen for her patient and careful editing. She completed this work while awaiting the arrival of her first child. May this child be blessed with a lifetime of sweet stories!

I am grateful to my friend David Behrman, whose family has provided the books to nurture generations of American Jews. David's wisdom, kindness, and commitment to Jewish life sustain the Jewish people in our time.

I am grateful to God for surrounding me with loving teachers and friends whose stories I am privileged to tell and retell. And to my family, who complete my own story. And especially to Nina, whose love and wisdom are God's greatest gifts to me.

Introduction

Telling a story is an act of spiritual generosity. It is a sharing of life. Stories convey our hopes, our dreams, our fears, our experiences, our wisdom, and our humor. It's not that we know stories or "have" stories or even collect stories. We *are* our stories. Our stories unite all the parts of our lives in a coherent whole. Stories make life meaningful. Just ask any stranger how he or she got here—and you'll get a story!

Years ago I started telling stories in both parts of my double job. By day I was the principal of a Jewish day school. By night I was the rabbi of a very large synagogue. On Friday mornings I'd tell stories to the nursery school kids, the kindergartners, and the students of the elementary school. Then I'd hunker down and write a sermon for the Friday-night service. One Friday I didn't get a chance to write the sermon. So I told the adults at the service the same story I'd told the schoolkids that morning. And they loved it. In fact years later, long after they had forgotten all my highbrow scholarly sermons, those congregants could retell that story. Somehow, stories remain with us long after everything else gets lost in the fog.

Jews have been telling stories for more than three thousand years. That makes for a lot of stories. Into those stories the Jewish people have poured their dreams and hopes and wisdom. In this volume I've gathered thirty-six of my favorites. To help you find just the right one, I have organized them according to six themes. In the section "What Really Matters in Life?" are stories about finding what is truly valuable. In "Doing What's Right" are stories celebrating the struggle to bring about goodness in the face of great resistance. The section "It's Up to You" tells about heroes who accept their role as God's partner in the process of healing the world. The stories in "Teachers and Friends" celebrate the power of teachers in shaping lives and touching the future.

"Hidden Truths" concerns the deeper wisdom concealed in our lives and the way we come to learn it. Finally, in "The Miracle of Jewish Life" are stories of the remarkable experiences of our people and faith. Then, at the end of the book, I've added a "Values Index," so that you can search for stories that embody a particular value, such as charity, faith, or friendship.

Following each story are a few questions for reflection and discussion. Keep in mind, however, that each story has meanings beyond those my questions may uncover. Engage in further thought and discussion and you may discover meanings of your own.

I did not compose these stories. Some of them I read in books. Some I heard at a Shabbat dinner table. Some I remember from my childhood. There are great scholars of Jewish stories who can tell us where a story came from, who first told it, and how its different versions developed. I have great reverence for such scholarship. But that's not my expertise. I'm interested in a story's power to teach. And so, to make the most of that power, I have taken the liberty of retelling the stories in my own way.

You may wish to read these stories to yourself. But I think they take on more life when they are read aloud. So find a friend, and share a story! And if you hear one that moves you, let me know. I can be reached at efeinstein@vbs.org.

Enjoy.

Rabbi Ed Feinstein
Encino, CA

PART ONE

What Really Matters in Life?

God has told you what is good and what is asked of you—
Only to do justice,
And to love kindness,
And to walk humbly with your God.

(Micah 6:8)

Paradise

Love stories are usually about young people sharing romance. This is a love story about older people who have shared a lifetime together and have come to understand what love and life are all about.

From the day Adam and Eve were exiled from the Garden of Eden, they lived together east of Eden, tilling the earth, raising children, and struggling to stay alive. After those many years of struggle, when their children were grown, Adam and Eve decided to take a journey before it was too late and see the world that God had created. They journeyed from one corner of the world to the other and explored all of the world's wonders. They stood upon the great mountains, trekked across the vast deserts, walked amid the mighty forests, and traversed the magnificent seas. They watched the sun rise over the endless wilderness and saw it set into the boundless ocean. All that God had created they beheld.

In the course of their journeys, wandering from place to place, they came upon a place that seemed so familiar. They came upon the Garden of Eden, from which they had been exiled on the very first day of their lives. The garden was now guarded by an angel with a flaming sword. This angel frightened Adam and Eve, who fled.

Suddenly they heard a voice, a gentle, imploring voice. God spoke to them: "My children, you have lived in exile these many, many years. Your punishment is complete. Come now and return to My garden. Come home to the garden."

Suddenly, too, the angel disappeared. The way into the garden opened, and God invited them in. But Adam, having spent so many years in the world, had grown shrewd. He hesitated and said to God, "You know, it has been so many years. Remind me, what is it like in the garden?"

"The garden is Paradise!" God responded. "In the garden there is no work. You need never struggle or toil again. In the garden there is no pain, no suffering. In the garden there is no death. In the garden there is no time—no yesterday, no tomorrow, only an endless today. Come, My children, return to the garden!"

Adam considered God's words. He thought about a life with no work, no struggle, no pain, no passage of time. And no death. An endless life of ease, with no tomorrow and no yesterday. And then he turned and looked at Eve, his wife. He looked into the face of the woman with whom he had struggled to make a life, to take bread from the earth, to raise children, to build a home. He read in the lines of her face all the tragedies they had overcome and the joys they had cherished. He saw in her eyes all the laughter and all the tears they had shared.

Eve looked back into Adam's face. She saw in his face all the moments that had formed their lives—moments of jubilant celebration and moments of unbearable pain. She remembered the moments of life-changing crisis and the many moments of simple tenderness and love. She remembered the moments when a new life arrived in their world and the moments when death intruded. As all their shared moments came back to her, she took Adam's hand in hers.

Looking into his wife's eyes, Adam shook his head and responded to God's invitation. "No, thank you," he said. "That's not for us, not now. We don't need that now. Come on, Eve," he said to his wife. "Let's go home." And Adam and Eve turned their backs on God's Paradise and walked home.

"It is not good for human beings to be alone."
—Genesis 2:18

When Adam was first created, he was alone. God placed him in Paradise, in Eden, but he was alone. God soon decided that Adam's solitude was a mistake. To be alone, even in Paradise, is no way to be. Human beings need one another. We need one another in order to share life's joys and sorrows. Sharing life, sharing love, is all the Paradise human beings ever need. It is Paradise even when it includes the sad and painful moments. Those are the moments when we truly understand the power of love to heal us and give us strength.

- Why don't Adam and Eve accept God's invitation to return to the garden?

- What experiences might Adam and Eve have shared that reinforced their love for each other?

- Do you know an older couple who have been together for decades and are still in love? If so, ask them if they understand this story. See what they say!

The Treasure

Ever dream of finding a buried treasure? Where might it be hiding? Sometimes the treasures we pursue turn out to be a lot less valuable than we imagined them to be. On the other hand, there are real treasures waiting for us in the places we least expect.

There once was a poor Jew named Yekel. Yekel was a dreamer. Each night he'd sit in his tiny hovel on a broken wooden chair at a battered wooden table over a glass of weak tea and imagine the treasures he knew were waiting for him somewhere. When he found his treasure, how his life would change!

Yekel's days and nights were filled with dreams of all that his treasure would bring. No longer would he live in the tiny broken-down hut, exposed to the cold wind and the rain. In his dreams he walked the halls of the fine home that would be his, a home with a roof that didn't leak like a sieve. He wandered through the broad rooms and up the fine staircases, with every floor covered with plush rugs and every window hung with lavish curtains. No longer would he wear the rags of a poor man. In his dreams he strolled the streets of the town in a proper suit, tapping the sidewalk with an elegant cane as he wished everyone a good-morning. In the sweetest of all his dreams, no longer would Yekel be dismissed as a poor, unaccomplished, foolish dreamer. When the treasure was finally his, he would have respect. He would be a man of position, importance, honor. The town's wise men would seek his counsel and revere his wisdom. But the years passed. And each night, Yekel would go to sleep, and each morning he'd awaken just as poor as he'd been the day before.

One night, Yekel had a dream. It was the most vivid, most powerful dream he'd ever had. In his dream he saw a bridge in the great city. Under the bridge, on the banks of the great river, was the treasure he'd waited his whole life to find. The dream was so real and the treasure so close that Yekel woke in the middle of the night, jumped from his bed, dressed himself quickly, grabbed his tools, and hurried to the great city. As dawn broke, he found the river and the bridge and the spot where the treasure was buried, just as the dream had shown him. He began to dig furiously.

After some time a policeman came by, a big-city policeman dressed in a stiff blue uniform with shiny brass buttons. The policeman peered down into the pit and, with a combination of curiosity and annoyance, asked the strange little man what he was doing. Why was he digging a pit beneath the bridge, beside the river, in the middle of the great city?

Yekel realized there was no sense lying about his intentions, so he pulled himself up from the pit, brushed himself off, faced the officer, and answered him directly. "I had a dream last night," he responded. "In the dream at this spot, beneath this bridge, beside this river, there was a treasure meant just for me!"

"You saw a treasure in your dreams? And so you came here to find it? All this for a dream? You believe in dreams? You're a fool!" laughed the policeman. "If I believed every dream I had, I'd be a fool too! Just last night I dreamed of a little Jew named Yekel who lives in a village not far from here. And what he doesn't know is that a great treasure lies buried beneath the floor of his own kitchen! But dreams are for fools, and I'm no fool!"

Hearing his name and mention of his treasure, Yekel quickly gathered his tools and ran home. Sure enough, when he dug up the floorboards of the very same kitchen he'd sat dreaming in night after night, Yekel found the treasure. And all that Yekel had imagined would come with the treasure was soon his. All those years, as he sat dreaming, the treasure was there, waiting for him just beneath his feet.

Yekel discovered that dreams are really not "over the rainbow." The most important treasures in our lives are right at home, waiting for us to discover them. Even more important, Yekel discovered that the treasures "out there" aren't real treasures. Spending our lives seeking such treasures—such goals—only leaves us poorer.

The Kabbalah, the Jewish mystical tradition, teaches that God is found in all things and in all moments. Our dilemma isn't that God is far away. It's that we think God is far away. The sixteenth-century mystic rabbi Moshe Cordovero of Tzfat taught, "The essence of divinity is found in every single thing." All it takes to know God is a change in the way we see the world. We don't have to travel far away to find truth, to meet God, or to experience holiness or happiness. Instead, we have to learn how to find the treasures that lie waiting in every moment and in every place.

- What treasures are hidden in your life right now?

- How can we become aware of those treasures and be grateful for them?

- How would such an awareness change us?

Diamonds and Potatoes

There are people who set out on their life journey with a clear idea of what they want, and they seem to get all of it and more. Most people, though, find themselves somewhere far from their original destination. Sometimes they land in a better place, sometimes in a worse place, but almost never in the place where they intended to land.

There once was a very poor man, who could provide his family with only the barest, most meager subsistence. The family ate potatoes for breakfast. They ate potatoes for lunch. And for dinner, potatoes once again. The monotony of the potatoes and the poverty of their lives wore on him and his family, but they could afford nothing else.

One day the man found an old book, and inside the book was a map showing the way to the Island of Diamonds. An island of diamonds! This must be the answer to all his problems. He would sail to the island, collect the diamonds, and return home rich as a king! And so he set out.

He borrowed a boat from a friend, took the map in his hand, and set sail to the Island of Diamonds. The seas were not easy to cross. Many times he thought he might be drowned by the storms and the waves. But finally one morning when he awoke, there on the horizon was a brilliant light—a light brighter than the sun. "It is the Island of Diamonds!" he thought, and he began to row furiously.

Soon the island came into view. And it was true. Right before him was a beautiful white beach, stretching as far as he could see, covered with brilliant diamonds. His heart leapt as he pulled his small boat ashore. "I'm rich! I'm the richest man in the world!" He jumped from the boat, carrying the dozen potato sacks he had brought from home, and began to fill the sacks with diamonds.

While he was busily packing the sacks with diamonds, the people of the island came down to the shore and stood watching him.

"What are you doing?" they asked curiously.

"What do you mean 'What am I doing?'" he replied in astonishment. "I'm gathering diamonds! I'm going to be rich—the richest man in the world!"

"Rich?" they laughed. "Those pebbles won't make you rich! Why, the whole island is covered with them; they're as common as rain."

"If these won't make me rich," he asked in utter puzzlement, "what will? What is it that you value here?"

"Well," the people responded, "there was once a fellow who found something much more valuable than those pebbles. He went up into the fields and came back with potatoes! Potatoes—now that's wealth!"

"Potatoes? Potatoes are wealth? I know more about potatoes than anyone! Just wait here." And with that he dumped the diamonds out of his sack and ran into the fields. Within fifteen minutes he had found a dozen potatoes. He returned to the crowd at the beach.

"Here—potatoes! And there are plenty more where these came from!"

"Potatoes!" the crowd repeated in awe. They carried the man on their shoulders from the beach and immediately declared him king of the island. All the luxuries of the island were brought to him. He was revered and worshipped. All he had to do was go into the fields and find a few potatoes each week.

After a year of this, he remembered his family back home and informed the islanders that he would soon be leaving. He set sail and faced the harsh trip home.

When he arrived in his home port, his family, friends, and neighbors turned out to meet him. Having been feared lost at sea these many months, he was greeted with tears and hugs. And finally his wife mustered the courage to ask, "Did you find the Island of Diamonds?"

"Did I find the Island of Diamonds! I became king of the Island of Diamonds!" he boasted.

Then, breathlessly, she asked him, "Have you brought us diamonds?"

"Diamonds? Heavens no!" he said. "I brought back something much more valuable than diamonds!"

"More valuable than diamonds? What could be more valuable than diamonds?" she inquired.

In response he hefted two huge sacks from the boat and spilled their contents on the dock.

"Behold," he announced gloriously, "I bring you *potatoes!*"

His wife tried to make sense of what she saw. "Have you lost your mind? You went to an island of diamonds, and you brought back potatoes? We have potatoes coming out of our ears!"

The expression of triumph quickly vanished from his face as he recognized what he had done. He'd gone to the ends of the earth to find diamonds and returned with potatoes.

Resigned to the fact that she would never see any diamonds, his wife took the potatoes home and prepared them for dinner. While she cooked, the children played with the empty sacks. And as they turned the sacks inside out, they found there, lodged in the mesh of the bag, a few small diamonds—diamonds that had not fallen out of the bag when the man emptied it on the beach. There were not enough to make the family rich. But those diamonds were worth enough to clothe and feed the family and, once in a while, provide something besides potatoes for their dinner.

The most serious spiritual problem most of us face is distraction. Hypnotized by the allure of some treasure, we depart from the pursuit of what is true to follow a fantasy. It takes great wisdom to resist that allure and great strength to pay attention.

The common Hebrew word for sin is cheit. *This term is from archery; it means "missing the mark; aiming but not hitting the target." Just as the archer may miss the mark not because he intended to but because he failed to concentrate, so most of our sins reflect a failure not of intent but of concentration.*

The Sh'ma, the statement of Jewish faith, concludes with the section from the Book of Numbers in which we are commanded to tie a fringe to our clothes as a reminder that we ought not be led astray by our hearts and eyes. Torah teaches what is worth pursuing and how to keep our eyes on the truth so that we might come home with real treasures and not just more potatoes.

- How did the man in the story end up with potatoes instead of the diamonds he went looking for?

- Is the story's ending a happy one? What does it say about what we end up with on our life journey?

- How can we learn to find diamonds in life and not get stuck with potatoes?

Turning Your Shoes Around

People look for ways to get into heaven. They believe heaven is far away. What if heaven were close by? What if all it took to get there was a different way of looking at things?

There once was a man who had given up on life. He found no joy in his work, his family, or his community. And so he prayed to God to let him leave this world. "Show me the way to Paradise!" he implored.

God asked him, "Are you sure that's what you want?"

The man replied, "I am sure with all my heart."

"Very well," replied God, who showed him the way to Paradise.

As it turned out, Paradise wasn't far away—just a few days' journey from his village. So late one afternoon he set out on his way. He walked until nightfall and then decided to rest beneath a leafy tree. Just before he fell asleep, it occurred to him that in the morning he might become confused and forget which was the way to Paradise and which was the way back to the village. So he left his shoes by the roadside, with the tips pointing toward Paradise so that in the morning all he'd have to do was jump into his shoes and continue on his way.

But sometimes unexpected things happen. Shoes get turned around. Was it an imp? Was it an angel? Was it just a squirrel? Who knows? But somehow the man's shoes got turned around. In the morning he rose feeling rested from his sleep, ate from the fruit of the tree, and prepared to set off on his journey. He went to the roadway, stepped into his shoes, and began walking—unaware that he was in fact returning home.

By noon he could see a village on the next hillside, and his heart leapt. "I've arrived in Paradise!" he thought. He ran down into the valley and up the hill, not stopping until he had arrived at the gates of the village.

"What a beautiful place is Paradise!" he thought. "My village was always so crowded, so noisy. This is different, so filled with life and joy!" He sat down on a bench in the square and witnessed the life of the village. He heard the songs the children sang at school and the sounds of the adults at work. He felt the vitality, the energy, and the love that filled the village. He sat in the square all day. In the evening he heard the joyful sounds of families reunited at home and smelled the meals that were being enjoyed by each family. And he began to feel hungry.

He thought, "Since Paradise looks so much like my village, I wonder if there is a street in Paradise like my street." And so he went to look. Just where he thought it might be, there's where he found it.

Then he thought, "I wonder if there is a house in Paradise like my house." And just where he thought it might be, there it was! Just as he was wondering at this marvelous coincidence, a woman came to the door—a woman who bore a striking resemblance to his wife. The woman called his name and asked him to come in for dinner.

His heart leapt. "They know me in Paradise! There is a place set for me here in Paradise!"

"I don't know what's in Paradise," the woman responded, "but your soup is getting cold at home. Come inside!"

He entered the house. This house in Paradise was nothing like his house in the village. That house was always crowded, cluttered, filled with commotion. This place was cozy and homey and filled with life. He sat at the table and ate the best meal he'd ever had. He complimented the woman on her heavenly soup. Afterward he went up to his bedroom and entered the deepest, most restful sleep he'd ever known.

In the morning the woman who looked like his wife handed him his tools and sent him to work. At first the man was incredulous. Who ever heard of working in Paradise? But then it occurred to him that even in Paradise there were tasks to be done. And he found that this work was different from the work he'd done before. Not dull or tedious, it filled him with a sense of purpose. And that night he returned to the same warm and loving home, the same kind woman, and more of her wonderful soup.

Do you know that in all the years that followed, no one could convince the man that he hadn't made it to Paradise! Every one of his days from then on was filled with more wonder, more purpose, more joy, and more life than the day before.

"It is good to give thanks to the Lord,
To praise Your name, O Most High.
To affirm Your love each morning,
And Your faithfulness each night."
—Psalm 92

Why does the psalmist wake each morning and go to bed each night with such a prayer? Did the psalmist live in the same world we live in? Didn't he see the ugliness and the evil in the world that we see? Didn't he ever wake up with a headache or go to bed with back pain?

Of course the psalmist lived in a world like ours. In fact, he probably lived in a world much worse than ours. But like the man in the story, he opened his eyes to a different way of seeing the world. The facts of his life remained the same. Only his attitude changed. And suddenly his life was very different.

• Where is Paradise—that place that has in it all that we need for happiness and satisfaction? And what does it take to find that place?

• In what ways can a person's attitude change?

• How does Torah teach us to point our shoes in the opposite direction and look at life differently?

The True Artist

*Our parents and teachers always tell us to do our best.
But few of us live up to that standard. Most of us get
through life without putting forth our best effort, fak-
ing it more often than not. This is a story about what
may happen when you take the easy way out.*

Once upon a time there was a king who built a great palace. It
was a magnificent palace, each room and each hall greater
and more impressive than the next. But there remained one hall
that was bare and undecorated. It was a long and narrow room
with high walls. "How should it be decorated?" wondered the king.

He decided to hold a contest, and he invited all the artists of
the land to submit their works. Then the king picked the two
artists whose works he liked most. He brought them to the great
hall and showed them its bare walls.

"I propose a contest," the king declared. "I give you one year
in which to decorate these walls. You may live here at the palace.
You may have all the paints and other materials you need. You
may hire all the assistants you require. You will paint this wall," the
king said to the first artist, pointing to the wall on his right, "and
you will paint that wall," he said to the second artist, motioning to
the wall on his left. "I will return in one year to judge your work.
Whichever one of you has done the better job I will reward with
riches, with honor, and with fame."

The two artists accepted the challenge.

The first artist set right to work. He gathered his ideas and thoughts, and he began to sketch and plan. He hired a crew of assistants and built a scaffold against the wall. By the end of the first month, he had finished his design, and he began to block it out on the wall.

As for the second artist, each day he would come to the great hall and stare up at his wall. All day he would sit and stare with a strange look on his face.

By the end of the second month, the first artist was well into his work. His design was sketched out on the wall, his paints were mixed, and fresh plaster had been prepared. As the third month ended, his design was taking shape on the wall.

And each day the second artist would come to the hall, sit down, and stare up at his blank wall.

As the months went by, the first artist's genius was becoming evident. The inspired design, bold figures, striking perspective, and magnificent colors and textures assured the artist that this was indeed his masterpiece—something unique, something never before created. His work filled him with excitement and enthusiasm.

And still each day the second artist would come to the hall, sit, and stare up at his blank wall.

The end of the year approached. The first artist was busy putting the very last finishing touches on his magnificent composition. His assistants were busy putting away the paints and other materials and breaking down the scaffold. On the last day of the last week of the last month of the year, the artist invited his assistants to a celebration. Only one task remained—to sign the magnificent work. He invited each of his assistants to sign it, and then the artist himself signed his name. He looked up at his creation and knew he had created something exceptional.

As the evening's celebration came to an end and he prepared to leave the great hall, he turned one last time to look at the opposite wall. It remained as blank and empty as it had been on the very first day of the contest. And there was the second artist, sitting and staring up at the wall as he had done every day of the year.

The next morning, the first morning of the new year, the two artists were summoned to the palace. The king asked them to wait in the antechamber as he entered the hall for the first time in a year.

The king looked upon the first artist's composition. His heart began to race, and tears came to his eyes. Never before had he seen a work of art so magnificent, so grand, so moving. Each figure and design had been executed with care, grace, and insight. He felt a distinct pride that he, the king, had sponsored and inspired so great a work of human creativity.

And then he turned and looked at the opposite wall. And there he saw something that shocked him. It was the same composition. Line for line, design for design, figure for figure, it was identical. Except on that wall he saw a king just like him staring back at him. Suspecting what the artist had done, he approached the wall and ran his hand across it. It was cold and hard and smooth. Yes, the artist had installed mirrors the length and breadth of the wall. Mirrors—so that everything that appeared on one wall was reflected by the other.

The king invited the two artists into the room. The first artist looked up at his work and felt his pride swell. Then he looked across at the other wall and became enraged.

"Who won?" they asked the king.

"Well, clearly both of you win!" the king replied. "Everything that appears on this wall also appears on that wall. The designs are identical. I declare the contest a tie, and each of you will be rewarded accordingly."

"But, no!" protested the first artist. "How can you? You see what he's done!"

"Silence!" commanded the king. "You must accept my decree! Return tomorrow to receive your rewards."

The two artists returned to the palace the next day—the first artist dejected and angry, the second elated and relieved. They were ushered into the great hall. And there in the middle of the hall was a mountain of gold—more gold than either man had ever seen or dreamed of in his lifetime.

The king spoke to the first artist: "You have created a masterpiece. Your work is profound and moving and beautiful. Your gifts are truly from God. And I am proud that I could be a part of so magnificent a work of art. You will therefore receive the reward you deserve. This gold is yours. There is enough to support you for the rest of your life. Now go and spread your gifts—bring beauty into the lives of others as you have brought it into my life."

The artist was surprised. He thanked the king again and again.

"Wait just a moment," the other artist interrupted. "You said we had both won, and we would both be rewarded. Where is my reward?"

"Oh, yes," the king responded, "I did promise that each of you would receive your due reward. And I intend to keep my word."

"So if he receives all this gold," the second artist asked, "where is my reward?"

"Why, look there," said the king, motioning to the reflection in the mirror. "Do you see *that* mound of gold there in the mirror? That is *your* reward, the reward that you deserve. Now take your reward, and leave my kingdom!"

The second artist looked up at the king in shock. And he slowly left the room.

Shortly before he died, the great philosopher Abraham Joshua Heschel gave an interview on television, at the end of which the reporter asked if he had a message for young people. Heschel replied that he wanted young people to realize that life is a work of art. We decide its colors, its textures, and its design. Therefore, it is up to every one of us to make of life a masterpiece. Unfortunately, lots of people give up their chance to create their masterpiece. Instead, they put up mirrors. They reflect what others expect, what others value, and what others want. They miss the chance to earn the true rewards of life.

- Why did the second artist put up mirrors? What are some of the ways in which people put up mirrors in their lives?

- Have you ever put up mirrors? Why or why not?

- What rewards did the second artist expect for his "work"?

The Tailor and the Prince

We all want to be rich and famous and beautiful because wealth, celebrity, and beauty make us feel important. But these qualities never really touch the essence of a person. The true value of a person is found far beneath the surface.

There once was a tailor who made exquisite clothes. Even the prince himself ordered his royal robes and uniforms from this tailor. The prince enjoyed the tailor's work so much that he came down to the tailor's village to thank him personally. He sat in the tailor's shop and watched with fascination as the tailor's fingers worked the thread so that the fabric magically came alive. Soon the two men had become friends—even though one was a simple, humble tailor and the other a great and powerful prince.

When the tailor's son was born, the prince sent a gift. A large box arrived at the tailor's home with a note attached:

> *My dear friend, in this box you will find the finest cloth in all the land. Put it away for now. When your son has grown into manhood, sew for him a cloak, and present it to him as a gift from his father's loyal friend, the Prince.*

The tailor and his wife were moved by the gift. They put the box in a safe place. And as people often do when they put something away, they soon forgot about it.

Years passed. One afternoon an imposing messenger arrived in the tailor's shop. The messenger presented an invitation for the tailor, his wife, and his son (now a young man) to attend a two-day royal ball in honor of the prince's birthday. At the bottom of the invitation, the prince had added a handwritten note:

My dear friend, royal business has kept me from visiting you for too long. Please share my joy on this special occasion. Your loyal friend, the Prince.

"A royal ball!" exclaimed the tailor. Filled with excitement, he lifted his wife to her feet and waltzed her around the shop. "We're going to the ball at the invitation of my friend the prince!" he sang.

The tailor's wife was more realistic. "My husband," she replied with thoughtful sadness, "I know how much your friendship with the prince means to you, but remember who we are. Royal balls are for lords and ladies, dukes and duchesses. We are common folk. We have no place there. What would we wear? At the royal ball, women wear gowns and jewels. All I have is a plain, simple dress."

"What difference does it make? The prince is my friend! We will go!"

On the first night of the ball, the tailor, his wife, and their son made their way to the palace. As they walked along the road, they were passed by the carriages of the nobles. As each carriage passed, the tailor's wife sighed. "Are you sure this is a good idea?" she would say.

"Yes, of course. I have an invitation signed by the prince himself!" was the tailor's reply.

They turned the last corner and stood before the palace, awestruck by its majesty and beauty. The edifice was all lights. Through the gates strolled lords and ladies, dukes and duchesses, in their gorgeous gowns and splendid uniforms, in their jewels and sabers and crowns.

The tailor's wife tried one last time to turn back. "My husband," she implored, "please, let's go home. We don't belong here."

"No!" he insisted. "We were invited. It would be a terrible insult to my friend the prince were we to refuse the chance to celebrate his birthday."

They approached the door. The nobles looked down at them in scorn. Some exclaimed, "Commoners!"

While his wife blushed in humiliation, the tailor strode proudly to the butler and presented his invitation. "I am a special friend of the prince," he declared.

"Indeed," replied the butler sarcastically as he eyed the tailor's simple clothes and workingman's shoes. "And where did you get this invitation?"

"What do you mean, 'Where did I get the invitation?' I received it from the prince himself!"

"Indeed," responded the butler. "I don't know how you came by this invitation, but you don't belong here. Just look at yourself. Anyone can see that you have no place here. Now please, sir, move away, and allow the guests to enter." The butler returned the invitation to the tailor and turned his back on the commoners.

"What do you mean?" shouted the tailor in exasperation. "I received this invitation from my friend the prince."

The tailor was beside himself. With his wife and son tugging at his sleeve, he tried one more time. He grasped the butler's lapel and shouted into his face, "Please, you must believe me!"

"Guards," the butler called angrily, "escort this commoner to the village!"

Two huge palace guards grabbed the tailor, carried him to the road, and threw him down the hillside. His wife and son ran sobbing behind. Bruised and humiliated, the tailor and his family arrived home.

His wife wouldn't stop crying. "Did you see the way they looked at us?" she asked.

The tailor's son was bewildered. "Why did they treat us that way, Papa?" he asked. "Why were they so cruel? After all, you are the prince's friend!"

The tailor was shaken. Then, suddenly, he remembered—and a vision flashed before his eyes. "The cloth! Of course—the prince's cloth! The gift we received when you were born!" he said to his son. "I'll sew it tonight, all night if need be. I'll make you a cloak. Tomorrow you will attend the ball in my place and wish my good friend the happiest birthday! Don't worry! Go to bed! By tomorrow you'll have your cloak!"

By morning the cloak was indeed complete. It was a master-piece. The cloth was lustrous. The colors were breathtaking. The design was exquisite. The workmanship was precise. When the young man tried it on, he looked resplendent. Glowing with pride, he stood taller than ever.

His father announced, "Tonight you will go to the royal ball and wish my friend the prince a happy birthday!"

When the boy thought of the ball, of the butler at the door, of the nobles, of the huge guards, his pride wilted. "How can I go, Papa? They'll never let me in!"

"Don't worry, my son, you'll go and celebrate with my friend the prince!"

The boy was not persuaded, but he wouldn't argue with his father. When evening came, he donned the cloak. His father shined his shoes to a gloss. His mother fixed his hair. And together they sent him to the ball.

Nervously the tailor's son walked slowly up the hill. As he turned the last corner and again beheld the palace—glorious with its lights and decorations—he began to tremble with fear. When he came before the butler, he timidly handed over the invitation. The young man braced for another onslaught of scorn and ridicule. Instead, the butler looked at the invitation and then looked the boy up and down.

"The prince's loyal friend?" said the butler. "Indeed! Welcome to the ball, young man."

"Welcome to the ball?" the boy echoed incredulously.

"Please, enter and greet the prince," responded the butler with a smile.

The tailor's son entered the palace. Breathlessly he took in the magnificent scene—the glorious ballroom hung with grand portraits of kings and emperors, magnificent women in beautiful gowns and opulent jewels, handsome men in dashing uniforms, dancing, music, tables laden with exotic foods. His heart leapt, for he had never seen anything so wonderful in all his life. And as he made his way through the room, he, too, was noticed. People smiled as they admired the handsome young gentleman in the marvelous cloak.

The tailor's son bowed deeply before the prince. In return the prince nodded to the young man. A footman took him by the arm and showed him to a table. Waiters came to serve him a fine wine in a golden goblet and delicacies on fine china. But as he sat taking in the wondrous scene, he felt a deep sadness. "If only my father could see this!" he thought. Then his sadness turned to anger as he remembered why his father was absent. His anger soon turned to fury.

There was a lull in the music. Abruptly the tailor's son stood up, removed his cloak, and in a booming voice asked, "Cloak, would you care to dance?" Revelers stopped and stared. They smiled and then looked on quizzically as the young man carried his cloak to the dance floor—and began to waltz. Holding his cloak as if it were his partner, one sleeve outstretched, he waltzed around and around the dance floor in great, exaggerated motions. "Cloak, you dance divinely!" he announced. By then everyone was watching this strange behavior.

As his dance came to an end, he bowed to the cloak and asked, "Cloak, would you care for some refreshment?" He walked his cloak to the table and, lifting a goblet of wine high in the air, poured it over the garment.

"Cloak, are you perhaps hungry?…Very well. Then eat!" He lifted a turkey leg from a platter and stuffed it into the sleeve of the cloak. The crowd froze. It was no longer a joke. The young man and his behavior were a disgrace, a mockery of the prince and his ball.

"Cloak," he announced, "we have not yet wished our host a happy birthday!" He approached the prince, bowed low before him, and proclaimed, "Your Highness, Cloak and I wish you a very special birthday!"

The prince stood and stared angrily at the tailor's son. "Who are you?" he demanded, "and why have you come to mock me and my guests?"

The tailor's son stared silently at the prince for a long time, his face contorted with anger and pain. Tears rolled down his cheeks. In a small voice he responded: "You invited my father to celebrate your birthday at the royal ball. You sent him a special invitation. You called yourself his loyal friend. That invitation meant more to him than any other invitation he has ever received. He showed it to everyone. He hung it in his shop window. He counted the days to the ball.

"Last night we came here: My mother, my father, and I came to celebrate with you. And your butler threw us out. My father didn't look like the rest of your guests so your butler threw him out of your house as if he were a dog. My father was humiliated, but he wanted somehow to send his birthday blessings to you. So he sent me back, dressed in this cloak made from the cloth you sent on the day I was born.

"I returned tonight because my father wouldn't hear otherwise. And something strange happened. I was allowed to enter your palace. Last night I was turned away, but tonight I was allowed in. Last night I was thrown out, but tonight I was offered food and wine. I am the same person; the only difference is this cloak! It's not me you have invited; it's the cloak! It's not my father, your friend, you want here—to dance and celebrate with you—it's this cloak! It's the cloak you have invited, the cloak's company you enjoy, the cloak's dancing and dining you wish to enjoy the sight of. So here—have the cloak!"

With that the tailor's son threw the garment at the prince's feet and stormed out of the ballroom and out of the palace.

The prince was stunned. Then he remembered. "The tailor! Where is my friend the tailor? That must be…" His shock turned to rage. "Send me the butler!" he bellowed. A moment later the butler was brought before the prince. "Last night my friend the tailor came with his wife and son, and you threw them out?"

"But, Your Highness, a…a…a commoner," the butler stammered in fear.

"Go now. Take my coach, and bring them here," the prince ordered sternly. "I don't care what they are wearing. Bring them

31

here so I can apologize. And see if you can find that strange boy as well."

Soon enough, the bewildered tailor and his wife were shown into the ballroom. He wore pajamas and she, a dressing gown.

The prince rose from his throne, approached the tailor and his wife, and bowed before them. "My old friend, please forgive me," said the prince, speaking from the heart. "Consider all our years of friendship and my loyalty to you, and please, please, forgive me, and please stay and celebrate with us."

The tailor was overwhelmed. The sudden appearance of the royal coach, the dazzle of the magnificent ballroom, the unprecedented sight of the prince bowing before *him*—and all with the tailor in his pajamas. "Why, of course," he sputtered, "and happy birthday."

The prince turned to the tailor's wife. "My lady, would you have this dance with me?"

"Yes, of course," she stammered.

"And where is that boy of yours?" asked the prince, a smile on his face. "I want to meet him properly."

The young man stepped out from behind a pillar. "Your Highness," he began, "I apologize. I should never have—"

"No, you are a brave boy," the prince corrected him. "I admire your character and loyalty. I could use a man like you in my service. Let us speak after the celebration, shall we?

"Now," the prince continued, lifting a goblet of wine and handing it to the tailor, "shall we celebrate, old friend?"

The music began. The prince swept the tailor's wife onto the dance floor as the tailor drank to the prince's health. And once again the royal ball came to life.

For the rest of their lives, the tailor and the prince remained loyal friends. The tailor's son entered the service of the prince, eventually becoming the prince's most trusted adviser—the prime minister. Everyone in the kingdom recognized him as the wisest man ever to wear the uniform of the prince.

It takes special insight to realize that our own value does not lie in our clothes—in our possessions—but in the qualities of our character. The Mishnah poses a wonderful question: When God created the world, God created herds of animals, schools of fish, flocks of birds, but only a single human being. Why? Wouldn't it have been so much more efficient to create a whole population at once? The Mishnah answers, "God created only one human being to teach the infinite value of each individual. So each individual can rightly say, 'The whole world was created just so I could come to be'" (Mishnah Sanhedrin 4:5).

- Why was the tailor's son so angry?

- What are some of the ways in which people are judged or measured, included or excluded?

- Why do we allow others to measure us by our appearance, our clothes, our possessions? Why do we judge ourselves by those same standards?

The Jester

Every child is asked, What do you want to be when you grow up? The response is usually some sort of profession: I want to be a lawyer, or an astronaut, or a scientist. But as we grow up, we realize there is a better answer: I want to be me—the most authentic, honest person I can be. Whatever work I do, I never want to forget who I really am.

There was once a king who ruled his kingdom with wisdom and compassion. As he approached the end of his days, everyone in the kingdom wondered who would be the next ruler. Would it be one of his children? An adviser? A general?

To keep the contenders from fighting over the throne, the king put his instructions in a letter, which was to be opened only on the day of his death. It named the person who would succeed him on the throne.

When that day arrived, the kingdom mourned its wise and caring leader. And then all eyes turned to the king's letter to see who would rule in his place. With great ceremony the prime minister opened the letter and read the instruction. Whom had the king chosen? Not one of his children, nor an adviser, nor a general. The king had chosen the jester. The jester would be crowned king!

The jester? Everyone in the kingdom thought this must be a joke. How could a fool be king? But such were the king's instructions. And so the jester was brought before the royal court. Royal retainers removed his jester costume and cloaked him in the robes of the king. They removed his jester hat and crowned him king. And they sat him on the royal throne.

At first the situation was awkward—for the new king as well as his kingdom. But over time it turned out to have been a brilliant choice. The jester was every bit as wise, as compassionate, and as insightful as the old king had been. He listened to everyone with care—advisers, generals, even the commoners of the realm. He treated everyone who came before him with respect and with kindness. He used his powers to bring peace and prosperity to his kingdom. To the amazement of all in the royal court, the jester came to be a superb ruler. And everyone in the royal court—indeed, everyone in the kingdom—came to love him.

There was a mystery surrounding the jester-king, however. Every so often he would retreat to a distant room in the palace, a room to which only he had the key. For a few hours he would lock himself in that room. And then he would return to the throne and resume his duties. Most members of the royal court assumed he went to the room to think, to meditate, or perhaps to pray. They accepted the mystery as part of their beloved king's life.

Once an ambassador came from a far-off land. The ambassador spent many hours with the king. He grew to appreciate the king's wisdom and his kindness. It was rare, he thought, for a king to listen as carefully as this king listened. It was unusual for a king to seek advice from everyone who appeared before him. It was remarkable for a king to care as deeply and to work as hard for the good of his subjects as this king did.

When the ambassador noticed that the king occasionally disappeared into his distant room, he wondered, "What does the king do in that locked room? Why does he go there? What is it in that room that helps him rule with such wisdom and kindness?" The ambassador just couldn't let go of the mystery. So one day when the king retreated to his room, the ambassador secretly followed behind. When the king closed the door, the ambassador crouched down and peered through the keyhole. There he took in the king's great secret.

In the privacy of the room, the king took off his crown and his royal robes and put on the costume of a jester. Around and around the room he danced the jester's dance, making funny faces and singing the silly songs of a jester. Then he stood before a great mirror and recited to himself: "Never forget who you are. You may look and sound and act like the king, but you are only the jester. You are only the jester pretending to be the king. Never forget who you are."

Now the ambassador understood it all. He understood the source of the king's deep wisdom. He understood that the king's kindness and greatness emanated from his humility. And now he knew the secret of the king's humility. This knowledge made the ambassador love the king even more deeply. He vowed his everlasting loyalty to the king. And he vowed to keep the king's secret.

Over the years the king and the ambassador grew close. One day when they were alone, the ambassador confessed what he had done and what he had seen. "I promise you on my life that I will never reveal your secret," he declared. "But there is one thing I have never been able to figure out: Of all the people in the royal court whom the old king could have chosen to succeed him, why did he choose you? Why did he choose the jester?"

The king smiled at his friend and replied, "And who do you think he was before he became king?"

Wisdom isn't about having all the answers. Wisdom means possessing the humility and patience to listen to each person's truth. That humility is the source of true greatness. Those who think they know it all, those who believe they have all the answers, betray what small people they really are. As Reb Zomah taught, "Who is wise? One who learns from all people. Who is respected? One who honors all people" (Pirkei Avot 4:1).

- Why do even great people need a dose of humility? How did humility make the jester-king a better leader?

- What happens to people who forget about humility?

- Do you think truly great people believe they are great? Or are we all just jesters pretending to be important? Explain.

PART TWO

Doing What's Right

✳

As God clothes the naked, you clothe the naked;
As God visits the sick, you visit the sick;
As God comforts the mourners, you comfort the mourners;
As God buries the dead, you also bury the dead.

(Talmud Sotah 14a)

It's Not My Problem

When we raise a glass of wine, we traditionally offer the toast l'chaim, *"To life!" It is interesting that the phrase is in the plural: It literally means "To lives!" This quirk of the Hebrew language reflects our understanding of being human. No life should be lived alone, in isolation. We share our lives with those we love and care for. Rooted in the lives of our loved ones and our friends, we thrive. Relationships are the very essence of life.*

Once there was a kingdom everyone called Paradise. It was called Paradise not because it was any more beautiful or any richer than any other place but because of the way the people who lived there cared for one another. In this kingdom, if a friend needed something from a friend, someone always stepped forward to help—without even being asked! If a neighbor needed something from a neighbor, someone would respond cheerfully and graciously without ever asking for anything in return. If a stranger needed something, people came forward to help with hospitality, generosity, and kindness.

All this was because of the wise king. The king knew that his subjects would treat one another the way he treated them. So he was always careful and attentive and helpful. If he couldn't help someone, he would at least listen and express his concern.

At last the king grew old, and he appointed his son, the prince, to rule in his place when the time came. Soon the king died, and the prince assumed the throne. But the prince was not wise like his father, nor kind, and he did not treat people the way his father did.

The royal ministers approached the prince and declared, "Your Majesty, we have a terrible problem. There is a famine in a certain corner of the land, and the people there are starving. We must do something!"

"They are starving?" said the prince impatiently.

"Yes, starving! They have no food to feed their children!"

"But I have plenty of food," responded the prince, biting into a big apple from the bowl of fruit before him. "If they are starving, I'm sorry. But it's not my problem!"

"Perhaps Your Majesty didn't understand. People are suffering, and they haven't any food. They'll die if we do nothing."

"Well I'm sorry, but it's just not my problem!"

The ministers shook their heads in disbelief and slowly walked away.

Just then another group of royal messengers approached the throne.

"Your Majesty, we have a terrible situation. A river has become poisoned, and the people who live along its banks have no water to drink! We must help them!"

"No water?" asked the prince even more impatiently as he poured himself a large glass of water.

"Yes, Your Majesty, there is no water! People are dying of thirst!"

"But I have plenty of water!" responded the prince, holding up his glass. "I'm sorry, but it's not my problem!"

No one in the royal court seemed able to move the prince. Every problem that was presented to him met with the same bothered look and the same response: "I'm sorry, but that's not my problem!"

Before long everyone in the kingdom was acting like the prince. When a friend needed help from a friend or a neighbor needed a hand from a neighbor, the one who was beseeched would look bothered and respond: "You need help? Well I'm sorry, but that's not my problem!" And since they refused to help one another, they certainly refused to help strangers.

Soon the kingdom had changed completely. It was no longer Paradise. It was a wilderness, a wasteland. Soon no one remembered the way things had been. No one remembered the Paradise that the kingdom once was. No one but Fisherman. Fisherman remembered the old king and the way things used to be. It hurt him that everyone had become as selfish as the young prince. If only he could remind the people and teach them. But what was one old fisherman to do?

Then one day he thought of a solution. He gathered all his money and bought tools and paint and materials. He set to work fixing up his old fishing boat. He would turn it into a yacht, the most beautiful yacht in the harbor.

Fisherman worked hard. Each day, people came by and admired his boat. "Hey, Fisherman," they'd say, "when you're done, will you take us for a ride on your yacht?"

"Sure!" he said. "Everyone will be invited!"

It took him a year to finish his work. When the yacht was ready, Fisherman made a huge sign and posted it for all to see. He invited everyone to come for a ride on the lake to celebrate the yacht's first voyage.

Everyone came that Sunday morning, even the prince! It was a splendid, clear day. The sun shone warmly, and the lake was calm. Fisherman guided his yacht out onto the lake. When he reached the middle, far from the shore, he dropped anchor and invited everyone to enjoy themselves. His guests brought out their picnic baskets and fishing poles, and everyone had a wonderful day on the lake. Late in the afternoon the wind picked up, and waves rocked the boat.

"Fisherman, can we head home now?" his guests asked.

"Sure," said Fisherman. "There's just one thing I need to do." He opened his toolbox and brought out a large hand drill. He walked to the exact center of the boat, positioned the drill on the hull, and began to drill.

"Say, Fisherman," people asked, "what are you doing?"

"I'm drilling a hole."

"But why are you drilling a hole?"

"Why? Because it's a nice day for drilling holes!" he responded nonchalantly.

"But, Fisherman, if you drill a hole in the boat, water will rush in, the boat will sink, and we'll all drown!" they said.

As he continued drilling, the passengers began to cry and beg: "Fisherman, please! Please, stop! You must stop!"

"Nope. It's my boat. It's my drill. And I'm going to drill this hole."

Someone remembered that the prince was on board. "Get the prince!" he shouted. "Someone get the prince! He'll save us!"

The prince swaggered over. No lowly fisherman was going to ruin his afternoon. He stood over Fisherman in his royal robes, and a hush came over the frightened crowd.

"Fisherman, what are you doing?" he asked in his deepest, most commanding voice.

"I'm drilling a hole," responded Fisherman, moving the drill around and around.

"Why are you doing this?" asked the prince in his deep, princely tone.

"Because I feel like it," responded Fisherman without even looking up at the prince.

"Fisherman, if you make a hole in the boat, the boat will sink, and we will all drown," the prince reasoned aloud.

"Uh-huh," acknowledged Fisherman.

Small beads of sweat appeared on the brow of the prince, and his voice lost its commanding tone and took on that of a sincerely worried man. "Fisherman," he said, "I command you to stop!"

Fisherman ignored him and kept drilling. The prince was quickly losing his composure. Gone were the royal tone and all the royal trappings. Instead, he was just another frightened man. "But Fisherman, what gives you the right to do this?"

Fisherman explained slowly: "It's my boat. It's my drill. And I'm going to make a hole. Now, please, move aside. You're blocking my light!" And he continued to drill.

The prince began crying and pleading, like everyone else. "Please, Fisherman, please," he begged. "I don't want to drown. I don't want to get eaten by fish. Please, Fisherman! Please!"

When the prince began to cry, Fisherman at last stopped drilling. Yet again a hush came over the crowd. Fisherman looked up at the prince. "You don't want the boat to sink? You don't want to drown?" Fisherman echoed the prince's pleas. Then Fisherman slowly repeated the terrible words that had ruined the kingdom: "Well, I'm sorry, but it's not my problem!"

The prince cried desperately, "What do you mean it's not your problem? Anyone can see that if I have a problem, you have a problem. And if you have a problem, I have a problem. If anyone has a problem, then everyone has a problem—because we're all on the same boat!"

He stopped. Like a man who had just figured out a great riddle, he repeated the words slowly: "If I have a problem, you have a problem. And if you have a problem, I have a problem. If anyone has a problem, then everyone has a problem—because we're all in the same boat! Anyone can see that!"

"Yes," said Fisherman, "anyone can see that!"

"Yes," said everyone on the boat, "anyone can see that!"

Fisherman smiled. "Now we can go home!" He pulled the drill up out of the hull, turned the boat around, and sailed safely back to the harbor.

The people who got off that boat were changed. Never, ever again would friend turn to friend or neighbor turn to neighbor or anyone turn to a stranger and say those terrible words. Instead, whenever a friend needed help from a friend or a neighbor needed a hand from a neighbor or a stranger needed some kindness, and whenever anyone came before the prince, he or she would hear, "Please, let me help you. Because if you have a problem, I have a problem. And if I have a problem, you have a problem. If anyone has a problem, then everyone has a problem. You see, we're all in the same boat!"

Once again the kingdom was Paradise.

★

"Hillel taught: 'If I am not for myself, who is for me?
But if I am only for my own self, what am I?
And if not now, when?'"
—Pirkei Avot 1:14

It is important for me to be for myself (and you for yourself). The question is, What is "myself"? Do the boundaries of the self include only oneself, or are others included as well? A fundamental truth of the Torah is that the self includes family, community, and, ultimately, the whole world. That is why if I am only for myself—if my concern is only myself—I destroy myself.

- Can you describe various situations in which people forgot this truth?

- Have you ever said, "It's not my problem"? If so, why did you say it?

- Why did Fisherman devise such an elaborate plan? What motivated him?

Heaven and Hell

When a child is only two years old, he or she learns the one word that changes everything: "me!" (or, sometimes, "mine!"). That's good for a two-year-old, but what happens when the child grows up and keeps on saying "me!" or "mine!"? What does it do to our world?

According to Jewish legend, every person has a soul, which is stored in Heaven until the moment when he or she is destined to be born. Then it enters the body and lives in the world. And when the time comes for a person to die, the soul leaves the body and ascends to Heaven. There the soul is judged; the person's life is reviewed. If the life included more good deeds than sins, more kindness and other virtues than evil, the soul is welcomed to Heaven. But if the life included more sins than good deeds, then the soul is sent to Hell for some time.

Once there arrived before the Throne of Judgment a soul whose goodness and sins were exactly balanced. No one could figure out what to do. The soul could not be sent on to Heaven; it wasn't worthy! And the soul could not be sent down to Hell; it wasn't guilty! After much deliberation it was decided that this soul would be given the opportunity to visit both Heaven and Hell and choose its own destiny. And so an angel took the soul on a tour of the two realms.

They journeyed first to Hell. Hell wasn't anything like what the soul had imagined. It was beautiful, a magnificent mansion set on a luxuriant lawn. In the mansion the soul was taken through halls and rooms, each more splendid than the next, and finally shown into a grand banquet room. In the middle of the room was a huge table laden with a feast the likes of which the soul had never dreamed of. There were delicacies of every sort piled high on rich golden platters, pitchers of fine wines and sweet nectars, tureens of savory soups, and desserts beyond description. It was, without doubt, the world's greatest feast.

A waiter entered and rang a small bell. Into the room came the inhabitants of Hell. To the surprise of the soul, they were emaciated—sickly, starved, and crying out in pain. How could this be, given such a feast? How could they live in the presence of such plenty yet look so hungry and forlorn? And then the soul saw how. The inhabitants of Hell could not bend their elbows. They could grasp at the fabulous food, but they could not put it in their mouths. And so they groaned and moaned in hunger and bitter frustration as the magnificent feast lay untouched before them.

The soul felt their anguish and begged to be taken away.

A moment later the soul entered Heaven. To his astonishment, it was identical with Hell. The same lush lawn, the same great mansion, the same elegant halls, even the same grand banquet room. As in Hell, the table was laden with platters and pitchers and plates of wonderful delicacies. When a waiter entered and rang the same small bell, the soul braced for another scene of frustration and torture. But when the inhabitants of heaven entered, they were different: They were healthy and joyful; they laughed and sang. Even more astonishing, the people of heaven suffered the same malady as their counterparts in Hell: They, too, were stiff armed, unable to bend their elbows. How, then, wondered the soul, were they so well fed, and why were they so happy?

As he watched, he beheld the one and only difference between Heaven and Hell: As the people of Heaven approached the table, instead of grasping the food for themselves, they turned and fed their neighbors. And in that way they enjoyed all the delicacies and all the delights of God's world.

And so may we.

On Yom Kippur, the holiest day of the Jewish year, we read from the Book of Isaiah: "This is the fast I desire....Share your bread with the hungry, and take the poor into your home; when you see the naked, clothe him, and don't ignore your own family" (58:6–7). God has no desire to see us piously fast and pray unless we turn to one another, feed the hungry, shelter the homeless, and clothe the naked.

There is only one thing that separates heaven—the greatest place—from hell—the worst of places. And that's the way we treat one another. If we are prepared to turn to one another in compassion, we can have heaven. If not, we make of our world a living hell. The choice is in our hands— or at our elbows!

- Have you ever been in a place that resembled this picture of hell—a place where everyone was out for himself and no one could get what she wanted? Describe that place.

- Why couldn't the people of Hell figure out what the people of Heaven understood? What attitude kept them from this discovery?

- Have you ever been in a place that resembled this depiction of Heaven? What one thing most contributed to its greatness?

The Holy Miser

The world is filled with angels. Angels aren't only heavenly creatures with wings. Angels are also people who do good things without asking for anything in return. They prefer to remain hidden and enjoy watching how their good acts bring the earth closer to heaven. Angels are everywhere; you just have to learn to see them.

They called him Reb Moishe the Miser. Reb Moishe the Miser was the richest man in the town. But he was also the meanest. When a beggar approached him and asked for a few pennies for food, Reb Moishe just grumbled and turned away. He turned away when the schoolmaster asked him to help the poor children of the town. When the leaders of the synagogue asked him for money to repair the shul's leaking roof, Reb Moishe simply shook his head. He even refused when the rabbi himself asked him to support the town's poor. Reb Moishe turned away everyone who asked him to give charity. He turned away from everyone's pleas for help. He turned away from doing anything for anyone.

So when Reb Moishe died—on a Monday—and the town was called to attend his funeral, everyone turned away.

Only the rabbi and the undertaker went to bury Reb Moishe. The undertaker prepared the grave. The rabbi said a few words of prayer. And together they buried Reb Moishe. No one cried for him. No one offered words of praise or comfort. When the rabbi and the undertaker had completed the burial, they, too, turned away.

That's when the strange things started happening. When the rabbi returned to his home, he found a poor man waiting for him.

"Rabbi, ten years ago, my wife got sick and I left my job to stay at home and care for her. When my savings ran out, I went to Reb Moishe the Miser to ask for help. He just groaned and turned away. But after that, every Monday morning I found a small bag filled with coins on my doorstep—enough money to pay for food and medicine. Every Monday morning for the past ten years— until this morning. This morning—no bag and no coins. Rabbi, I wonder if you could help me."

The rabbi listened to the story. Then he opened his purse and gave the man the coins he needed.

The next day the schoolmaster came to see the rabbi.

"Rabbi, for the past twelve years, every Tuesday morning when I arrived at the schoolhouse, there would be a bag waiting for me. Every bag contained a surprise. Sometimes it contained a coat for a child whose family was too poor to afford a new coat for the winter. Sometimes there was a new book for a child who loved to read. Sometimes there was a treat for every student. Once, just in time for Hanukkah, there was a purse filled with coins. Rabbi, I don't know who left that bag every Tuesday, but somehow that person knew exactly what I needed every week, and that's what he left. But this morning—no bag and no surprise."

On Wednesday it was a poor widow, who had found a bagful of coal for her furnace every Wednesday throughout the winter for the past fifteen years. But not this Wednesday.

On Thursday it was the baker, who had found a purse filled with coins and a list of people to whom he was to deliver a Shabbat challah—every Thursday for twenty years. But not this Thursday.

And on Friday the *shammes*, the caretaker of the synagogue, reported that every Friday for as long as he could remember there had been wine for Kiddush, candles for Shabbat, and food for any poor person who might spend Shabbat in the synagogue. Those items had just appeared by magic—but not this Friday.

By the time Shabbat arrived, the rabbi had figured it out. He stood during the Shabbat prayers and announced that the entire community must accompany him to the cemetery at the end of Shabbat to offer an apology to Reb Moishe the Miser, who had been quietly caring for the sick, the hungry, the poor—for every needy person in the town—for all these years.

As Shabbat ended, the entire town gathered at the grave of Reb Moishe the Miser. The rabbi spoke about holiness. He said: "As God is holy, we are commanded to be holy. How can we, mere human beings, be just like God? Just as God clothed Adam and Eve, we are commanded to clothe and protect the vulnerable. Just as God comforted Abraham, we are commanded to comfort the sick. Just as God fed Israel in the desert, we are commanded to feed the hungry. Just as God buried his friend Moshe the holy prophet, we are commanded to bury our friend Reb Moishe the Holy Miser."

That night the rabbi awoke to find his bedroom filled with light. Right there before him was the shining likeness of Reb Moishe.

The rabbi fell to his knees and pleaded, "Reb Moishe, I beg you, forgive us. We did not know all that you had done!"

Reb Moishe smiled a sweet smile. It was the first time the rabbi had ever seen Reb Moishe smile. "Of course you did not know," he said. "I didn't want you to know. I did what I did in secret so no one would feel obligated to repay me. All that I did gave me so much joy. You need not apologize to me. But I do need you to perform one favor for me: Go to my home, and look under my bed. There you will find a box filled with all my money. Use it to carry on my work—for the poor families, the widows, the children, the synagogue. Use all the money to bring happiness and light to this town."

"Certainly, Reb Moishe," the rabbi replied, "I will do as you ask." And then the rabbi grew bolder. "May I ask you a question, Reb Moishe?" And without waiting for a response, he proceeded: "What is it like there, in the other world? What is heaven like?"

"What is heaven like? It's paradise! God's paradise. It's almost perfect."

"Almost perfect?" questioned the rabbi. "What's missing from God's paradise?"

"Here God cares for every soul. So here there is no one for me to take care of, no one to help. If only I could care for another soul—that would make it perfect!"

So much of modern culture is about getting. We seem to have forgotten that there is a special joy in giving, not because it brings us recognition but because it elevates us, bringing us closer to God. The aspect of God that we can know best, taught the philosopher Abraham Joshua Heschel, is God's selfless caring. As we cultivate a commitment to caring, we become holy. As the Talmud tells us, "Rabbi Elazar taught, 'Those who do deeds of charity and justice, it is as if they filled the entire world completely with loving-kindness'" (Talmud Sukkah 49b).

- Have you ever met someone like Reb Moishe, someone who does good for others without asking for recognition or reward? Why does he or she refuse the reward for doing good? What does the person get out of it?

- It is said that a person who is willing to do good without any reward is capable of saving the whole world. Is that true? Why or why not?

Day and Night

If there were just one thing we could change in the world to bring the world closer to perfection, what would it be? If there was just one change we could make in our character to bring us closer together, what would it be?

A rabbi once asked his students, "How do we know when the night has ended and the day has begun?"

The students thought they grasped the importance of the question. There are, after all, prayers that can be recited, and rites and rituals that can be performed, only at night. And there are prayers and rites and rituals that belong only to the day. It is therefore important to know when night has ended and day has begun. It is important to get the prayers and rites and rituals correct.

The brightest of the students offered an answer: "Rabbi, when I look out at the fields and I can distinguish between my field and the field of my neighbor, that's when the night has ended and the day has begun."

A second student offered his answer: "Rabbi, when I look from the fields and I see a house and I can tell that it's my house and not the house of my neighbor, that's when the night has ended and the day has begun."

A third student offered an answer: "Rabbi, when I see an animal in the distance and I can tell what kind of animal it is, whether a cow or a horse or a sheep, that's when the night has ended and the day has begun."

A fourth student offered yet another answer: "Rabbi, when I see a flower and I can make out the colors of the flower, whether they are red or yellow or blue, that's when night has ended and day has begun."

Each answer brought a sadder, more severe frown to the rabbi's face—until finally he shouted, "No! Not one of you understands!

"You only divide! You divide your house from the house of your neighbor, your field from your neighbor's field; you distinguish one kind of animal from another; you separate one color from all the others. Is that all we can do—divide, separate, split the world into pieces? Isn't the world broken enough? Isn't the world split into enough fragments? Is that what Torah is for? No, my dear students, it's not that way, not that way at all!"

The shocked students looked into the sad face of their rabbi. One of them ventured, "Then, Rabbi, tell us: How do we know that night has ended and day has begun?"

The rabbi stared back into the faces of his students, and with a voice suddenly gentle and imploring, he responded: "When you look into the face of the person who is beside you and you can see that that person is your brother or your sister, then finally the night has ended and the day has begun."

When will the long night of human suffering and exile come to an end? And when will the daybreak of Redemption come to us? Only when we open our eyes and really see one another. Only when we see how closely connected we are to one another. Only then will nighttime end and the day begin. And so we pray: "Lord, our God, we hope for a time when Your glory will be revealed to us, when all the world's evil will be removed, all the world's idols destroyed, and the world will be repaired and turned into a domain of God" (Aleinu l'Shabei'ach, *from the Siddur*).

- Were the students' answers wrong? Why did the rabbi get angry?

- What question were the students answering? What question did the rabbi want answered?

- What kind of attitude does it take to look into the face of another person and see him or her as a brother or a sister? How would that attitude change the world?

Please Don't Eat That Sheep!

*The Bible isn't about holy, perfect people. It's about
ordinary, flawed people struggling to be good and to
share God's dreams. The Bible is an invitation to join
God in making a world of goodness, even if we have to
do it one tiny step at a time.*

When God created human beings, God gave them the
freedom to choose. A dog will always be a dog, and a cat
will always be a cat. But a human being can decide to be good or
evil, to love or hate, to create or destroy.

It was God's hope that human beings would be God's partners
and share God's dream of a world of goodness. But human beings
chose otherwise. They filled the world with violence, cruelty, and
evil. So filled with evil was the world that God regretted ever having
created human beings. God decided to destroy it all—the whole
world and all its evil.

But just before that destruction, God noticed one man. That
one man, Noah, was a righteous, good person, a man worth saving.
For Noah's sake the world was worth saving. So God changed the
plan. God decided to destroy all the evil and start the world again
with Noah as its father.

But the truth is that although Noah had much goodness in
him, he wasn't ready to teach the world to share God's dream of
goodness. There was something Noah needed to learn first.

God spoke to Noah and told him to build an ark and save the
world from the coming flood. Noah followed God's instructions.
He built the ark, gathered all the animals, and on the day the rain

started, Noah brought them all on board and closed the ark. He thought he had fulfilled his mission. Little did he know that his task was just beginning.

As soon as the voyage began, Noah's son came running to his father. "Father, come quick!" he said. "The lion is about to eat the sheep! Come quick!"

So Noah hurried to the lion's place in the ark, and sure enough, there was the lion ready to have the sheep for lunch.

"Wait!" screamed Noah. "You can't do that!"

"What do you mean I can't do that?" asked the lion. "It's lunchtime, I'm hungry, and I eat sheep for lunch almost every day!"

"But not today," Noah explained, trying to reason with the lion. "Today I'm asking you, please, don't eat that sheep! You see, I have only two of them. And if you eat them both, there will be no more sheep on earth ever again."

"But it's my nature to kill and eat. I'm a carnivore. That's who I am. And I love sheep!" responded the lion.

"Yes, I know," answered Noah. "But for now, while we share this ark, you must put that part of yourself away. While we share this ark, you must protect the life of every other living thing; you cannot kill your fellow passengers."

"Then what shall I eat?" asked the astonished lion.

"How about straw?" Noah proposed.

"Straw? Yuck!" The lion was truly appalled.

"Just until this is all over and we've left the ark. Eat straw," Noah instructed the lion. "In return, I will tell the world of your generosity, and all the world will recognize in you the quality of strength, a quality they regard highly. You'll be revered as the king of beasts!"

"Very well," agreed the lion, feeling very regal. "I'll have straw for lunch."

Just then another one of Noah's sons came running. "Father, come quick," he panted. "It's the elephants! They're playing tag! They're going to capsize the ark! You've got to come and stop them!"

So off Noah went to keep the elephants from capsizing the ark.

"But we're playful creatures; it's our nature," complained the elephants when Noah asked them to stop. "How can we stop playing?"

"Just until we're home, stop playing, and I will announce to the world how wise the elephant is."

"Very well, no more games until we're home," agreed the elephants.

Next it was the monkeys, who playfully stole everyone's food and hid it.

"It's our nature to steal things. That's how we have fun! Besides, we're just kidding! We mean no harm."

"I appreciate that," replied a frustrated Noah, "but just until our voyage is over, you must not steal. Stealing makes everyone on the ark angry and sets us against one another. Refrain from stealing, and when we are home again, I will make sure the world knows how much laughter you bring to us all."

"Very well," agreed the monkeys. "No stealing."

The pigs presented a special problem. Pigs make a mess everywhere. They never clean up after themselves. "What can we do?" they pleaded helplessly with Noah. "That's just the way God created us!"

"Of course that's the way God created you," Noah responded. "But just for now try to be just a little better than that! Try to practice courtesy even if it isn't natural to you. You can do it if you try!"

The pigs looked at each other in dismay. "Courtesy? We're pigs! But for you, Noah, we will try courtesy. We'll be courteous pigs!"

And so it was with every creature on the ark. Every creature needed to learn to give up a piece of its nature in order to share the ark and complete the voyage. The lion gave up killing; the elephants, playing; the monkeys, stealing. The pigs learned courtesy. The mosquitoes, who normally bite and annoy every other creature, learned to respect others' privacy. The roosters promised not to awaken everyone early in the morning. And the bats promised not to frighten everyone else by flying around in the dark.

Noah was successful with every creature until he came to the most difficult and most complicated one of all, the human being. People, it seemed, exhibited all the worst behaviors of all the other animals: killing, playing, stealing, messing, annoying, irritating, and destroying. But although people might act like the other animals, Noah discovered, they possessed one quality that made them special. Noah could persuade every animal to give up one element of its nature, but no animal could ever be more than an animal. People, however, can be more than animals, more than their nature—people can be more than people. They can reach up and become loving, kind, and good, like God.

That's what we learn from Noah's time in the ark.

"What are human beings, O God, that You know them,
Or the children of humanity, that You are mindful of them?
But You have made them but little lower than the angels
And crowned them with glory and with honor."
—Psalm 8:5–6

What defines a human being? What makes us special among all the creatures of the world? It is that we can transcend ourselves. We can go beyond the boundaries of our birth and upbringing, our nature and our habits. We can choose to rise up and share the dreams of God.

- Noah learned to be a good man. How did he do that?

- What did Noah learn from the animals on the ark?

- Can we give up parts of our nature in order to live together? How do we learn to do that?

Elijah's Gifts

If you touch the palm of a newborn baby, the baby's hand will close around your finger. Grasping is a reflex we are all born with. Sharing isn't a reflex. Learning to share takes a lifetime. But sharing is what brings us closer to God.

There once was a man who lived a life of kindness and generosity. He looked upon every bit of his fortune as a gift from God and shared with all who were in need. So good was his life that when he died, it was decreed in heaven that each of his three sons should receive the one wish of his heart as a reward for his father's kindness. Elijah the Prophet was dispatched to offer each of the brothers his wish.

Elijah approached the eldest brother and offered him any wish of his heart. The young man didn't hesitate even for a moment before he answered: "What I want most is wealth and power and respect. I want to be the most important man in all the land."

"Very well," replied Elijah. "It is done."

Upon arriving home, the eldest brother found an old boot on his doorstep. As he was about to throw the old boot away, he saw that it was filled with gold coins. He took the boot into his tiny home and spilled out the coins on his bed. As he began to celebrate his good fortune, he saw that when he put the boot down, it filled again with gold coins. So he spilled the contents of the boot again. And again, it filled up with coins. And so it was, until he became the wealthiest man in the land. He built a great mansion and purchased many farms. The people of the town came to him for advice, and soon he was elected mayor. He was honored as the most important man in the land—just as he had wished he would be.

Elijah approached the second brother and offered him any wish of his heart. The second brother reflected for a moment and then answered: "I've always sought wisdom and understanding and knowledge. I've always wanted to know the answers to all the great questions. That is my wish. Teach me the answers, the secrets, to all the world's questions. I wish to be the wisest, most learned man in the land."

"Very well," replied Elijah. "It is done."

Upon arriving home, the second brother found a package wrapped in plain paper and tied in twine. He brought the package into his home and unwrapped it. Inside he found an old book bound in leather. He began to read the book and discovered in it all the answers to all the questions he had ever asked. And anytime he arrived at a new question, he found a new chapter in the book that answered his question. Soon he was the wisest, most learned man in the land—just as he had wished he would be.

Finally, Elijah went to the home of the youngest brother. The brother welcomed him warmly, invited him into his home, and prepared him a cup of tea. Elijah offered the youngest brother any wish of his heart.

The young man shook his head and thought for a long time. At last he replied, "I really have enough. There is nothing I really need. I have no wish, except to be happy in my life."

"Very well," replied Elijah. "It is done."

"What is done?" asked the young man. "What did I wish for?"

That evening as he sat down to his supper, there was a knock at the youngest brother's door. There stood an older man.

"Dear sir, I'm sorry to bother you. We are travelers. Our wagon has broken its wheel. It will certainly take some time to repair. May we stay a while in your barn, until the wagon can be fixed?"

"It's too cold to stay in the barn. Come into my home! You must be hungry. Sit with me at my table and share my supper!

Tomorrow we will see about fixing your broken wagon. But tonight you'll stay here. How many are you?"

"Just two, my granddaughter and I." Just then a beautiful young woman emerged from the wagon.

That night the grandfather and granddaughter shared supper with the youngest brother. After the meal they sipped tea. The grandfather recited stories of his many travels. The youngest brother spoke of his good and generous father. The granddaughter recounted stories from the books she had read.

Soon the youngest brother felt close to the granddaughter, and she felt close to him.

The next day the youngest brother set about repairing the broken wagon wheel—but he left one piece unfinished so that the old man and his granddaughter would have to spend another evening in his home. They shared another fine supper and another evening of stories. And again the next day he almost completed the job but left one task undone.

Soon enough the youngest brother had fallen in love with the stranger's beautiful granddaughter.

When the wagon was finally repaired, the young man begged the grandfather to stay, and he asked permission to marry the man's granddaughter. The grandfather recognized what a fine person the young man was and joyfully consented. Soon the youngest brother was the happiest man in the land—just as he had wished to be.

All three brothers received their wishes. But did they use them the way their father had taught them? The father was kind, generous, and good. He recognized that his fortune was a gift of God, and he graciously shared all that he had. Would his sons use their gifts in the same way? Elijah the Prophet was dispatched to find out.

He came to the eldest brother disguised as a poor beggar. "Please sir," begged Elijah, "a few pennies for bread, that's all I ask. It is said that you are the wealthiest, most important man in all the land. God has blessed you with so very much. Would you please spare a few pennies for bread?"

The brother looked at the beggar in disgust. "Get away from me, you filthy creature!" he commanded. "I owe nothing to worthless creatures like you! Go and make your own way in the world! I worked hard for my fortune! Go and find your own!"

At that Elijah removed his disguise. "You worked hard for your fortune?" he asked. "It wasn't your hard work that earned this fortune but your father's kindness and generosity. He never failed to share his good fortune. He fed every beggar who ever came to his door. But you have not learned his kindness. You don't understand that wealth is a gift to be shared. And therefore your fortune will soon be lost."

The eldest brother ran to find his magic boot. As always, it was filled with gold coins. And so he scoffed at Elijah's words: "You can't take my fortune!" But when he emptied the coins from the boot, it did not fill up again. Soon his foolish selfishness caught up with him, and he lost all his fortune. Those who respected him so highly when he was wealthy turned their backs on him. And he returned to the way he had been.

Then, disguised as a poor student, Elijah visited the second brother. "Please, sir," he said, "teach me! It is said that you are the wisest, most learned man in all the land. God has blessed you with such knowledge. Could you spare a few moments to teach a poor student who seeks only the truth?"

Like his elder brother, the second brother looked away in disgust. "Get away from me, you ignorant creature!" he said. "Can't you see that I have no time for fools like you! I worked hard to earn wisdom. Why would I share what I know with a simpleton like you?"

At that Elijah removed his disguise. "You worked hard to earn wisdom?" he asked. "What exactly do you know? Your father shared his wisdom generously. And he never failed to share his time; he taught anyone who came to him seeking understanding. But you never learned the lessons of his kindness. You never learned that wisdom is a gift to be shared. Therefore your learning will soon be lost."

The second brother scoffed at Elijah's words. "How can my learning be lost?" But just to make sure, he ran to find his magic book. And when he found it, he was shocked to discover that its pages were blank. Soon his selfish foolishness caught up with him, and he forgot all he had learned. And he returned to being as he had been.

Finally Elijah visited the youngest brother disguised as a traveler. Having met the selfishness and foolishness of the first two brothers, he was worried about what he'd find. He knocked at the youngest brother's door one night as the family was sitting down to supper.

"Dear sir," said Elijah, "I'm sorry to bother you. I am a traveler. My wagon has broken its wheel. It will certainly take some time to repair. May I trouble you by staying a while in your barn, until the wagon can be fixed?"

"No!" replied the brother. Elijah feared that his concerns were justified.

But the brother continued, "Not in the barn! Come into our home! You must be hungry. Sit with us at our table and share our supper! Tomorrow we will see about fixing your broken wagon, but tonight you'll stay here with my family."

The youngest brother invited Elijah into his home and sat him at the table beside his wife and her grandfather. Before the meal the youngest brother covered his head and recited a prayer: "Let us thank God for all the gifts that are ours. For the bread we eat, for the love we share, for this warm home, and for our guest who has come tonight to share our meal. For all the happiness that God has brought us, blessed is God who brings bread from the earth."

At that Elijah removed his disguise. "You have learned the lessons your father taught. All his kindness, all his wisdom, and all his generosity are yours. Therefore, it has been decreed that all the gifts your brothers wasted shall be yours: the fortune of your eldest brother and the learning of your second brother. And your gifts shall be doubled and doubled again."

And so they were. The brother lived a long life with his wife, who brought him happiness, and with their many, many children. And each child was given the gifts of kindness, generosity, and goodness.

The great sage Rava taught, "When a person is brought before Judgment in the next world, he or she will be asked: 'Did you do business with honesty? Did you find time for Torah learning? Did you give yourself to your family? Did you keep hope in the future alive?'" (Talmud Shabbat 31a). These questions aren't only for the dead. They are the questions we should ask ourselves in life. These are the qualities that make for a complete life: honesty, learning, love of family, and hope. They are the things we should be seeking, wishing for, and working toward.

- How hard is it to learn how to share?

- According to the story, what must we remember in order to share what we have?

- Are there gifts of life that we lose if we don't share?

PART THREE

It's Up to You

✳

*When God created Adam, God showed him all the trees
in the Garden of Eden and said, "See how beautiful and perfect
are My creations! All that I have created, I created for you.
Therefore, be careful: Do not abuse or destroy My world.
For if you abuse or destroy it, there is no one to
repair it after you."*

(Midrash Kohelet Rabbah 7:20)

The Clock

The clock can be an enemy. It is always yelling, "Go faster! Work harder! Get more done today!" But some days the clock says something else, something sweeter. Some days it says, "You've done a good job; you've spent your time well." In the end, how we think about ourselves has much to do with how we read the clock.

All over the Jewish world the Jewish people suffered the agony of exile. Life was terribly hard, and God's Messiah seemed far away. But not in Lublin. Not in the home of the great Hasidic master Rabbi Yitzhak Ya'akov, the Seer of Lublin.

Once a visitor asked one of the disciples of the Seer, "If your master is so powerful and so wise, why doesn't he bring the Messiah and put an end to all our suffering?"

"A good question," replied the Hasid. "But you see in Lublin, in the court of the Seer, we have so much ecstasy, so much joy, for us it is as if the Messiah had already arrived!"

In truth the Hasid knew that the Messiah had not yet arrived. But he believed the arrival would come any day. All that was needed was the right depth of concentration in prayer, the right perfection of religious practice, the right mastery of the holy books, and the Messiah would appear and redeem the world. Every Saturday evening the disciples of the Seer would extend their Sabbath, often late into the night. A tradition taught that the Messiah would come as the Sabbath was ending, so as to extend the Sabbath rest and joy into eternity. So the disciples of the Seer sat for hours on Saturday nights, singing and praying, refusing to accept the inevitable end of the Sabbath and the arrival of another mundane workweek.

When the Seer of Lublin died, his disciples gathered to divide his worldly goods. One Hasid got his books. One received his Kiddush cup. Another was given his *tallis*. There remained one humble Hasid. He was given the master's clock.

That last Hasid had before him a long journey home, for like many of the Seer's disciples, he had come from far away to learn the holy secrets of the Seer. On his way home this Hasid stopped at an inn to rest for the night. When he realized that he had no money with which to pay the innkeeper, he had no choice but to offer the rebbe's clock as payment. The innkeeper accepted the clock and installed it in one of the rooms of the inn.

Years later another of the Seer's Hasidim passed by and stayed at the same inn. All night long he could not sleep. All night the innkeeper heard the restless footsteps of the Hasid pacing the floor—back and forth, back and forth.

In the morning the innkeeper approached the weary Hasid. "You didn't sleep at all last night! I heard you pacing all night long. Was there something wrong with the room? Was the bed too hard or the pillow too soft?"

The Hasid was agitated. His face betrayed his fear. He grabbed the innkeeper by his lapels: "It was the clock. The clock in the room kept me up all night. That is no ordinary clock. Where did you find it? How did you come by it?"

The innkeeper related the story of his visitor years before.

"I knew it!" responded the Hasid. "This clock belonged to the Holy Seer of Lublin. It is a holy clock. You see, all the clocks in the world mark time from the past. All clocks measure where we've come, how far we've journeyed from our beginnings. This clock is unique. This clock ticks from the future. It tells us how much more there is to do before Redemption can be realized. Every time I lay down to rest, the clock said, 'Get up. How can you rest? Get to work now! The Messiah is so near! Redemption is waiting for you. It's waiting for you to bring it!'"

That's how the story was told in one corner of Lublin, by one faction of the Seer's disciples. But in another corner it was told differently:

In the morning the innkeeper approached the Hasid.

The Hasid was excited, his face aglow. He grabbed the innkeeper by his lapels and swung him about in a joyful dance. "It was the clock…" And when the innkeeper explained how he had come by the clock, the Hasid exclaimed joyfully, "I knew it! This is the holy clock that belonged to the Holy Seer! Every clock in the world tells us how much of our lives has passed and how much closer we are to the grave. But not this clock. This clock measures time from the future, from the Redemption. This clock ticks toward the day the Messiah will come and bring us peace! Every time I lay down to rest, the clock ticked one more tick, and I could do nothing but jump up and dance and celebrate when I realized how close we are to Redemption and to the Messiah's arrival!"

Some people measure themselves by looking at the past. They see that the times behind them were better and lament how far they are from the good old days. For others the clock is a reminder of what's ahead and what they have to do to get there. The future beckons and invites their energy.

There are cultures that imagine the Golden Age only in the past. They long for a return. They view the future with skepticism. Others imagine the best days ahead. It's all a matter of how you read the clock.

- In each version of the story, what keeps the Hasid awake throughout the night?

- What's the difference between an ordinary clock and the Seer's clock?

- What's the difference between the two versions of the story?

Splitting the Sea

What does it take to be a hero? Heroes aren't always famous, and they're not necessarily brave. To be a hero is to give your whole self to something of great importance. How can we become heroes?

The most exciting, most suspenseful moment in the entire Torah has to be the story of the splitting of the Red Sea. Everyone remembers the story we tell each year at the Passover seder:

The Israelites escape from Pharaoh's cruel slavery after the terror of the Ten Plagues. They hastily escape from Egyptian bondage, fleeing to the desert without even taking the time to let their bread rise. And then, as they camp on the banks of the Red Sea, Pharaoh's heart is hardened one last time, and he resolves to pursue the Israelites and slaughter them. His charioteers come charging across the desert.

The Israelites find themselves trapped, the impassable sea on one side, the charging army of Pharaoh's charioteers on the other. They cry bitterly to Moses, who raises his eyes to God in prayer. God admonishes him: "This is not the time for prayer. Command the Israelites to move forward. And lift up your staff and hold out your arm over the sea and split it, so that the Israelites may march into the sea on dry ground" (Exodus 14:15–16).

According to the Torah, Moses did exactly that. The people crossed in safety. And when Pharaoh's troops followed them, the sea returned and drowned them all. Thus Israel was freed once and for all from the cruelty of Pharaoh. This is the greatest story of redemption in all our literature.

But the rabbis of a later generation read the story more critically. They were disturbed that in the Torah's story, God does all the work while the Israelites passively watch the spectacle of redemption. God sends Moses and tells him what to say. God brings the plagues and hardens the heart of Pharaoh. God brings the Israelites out of Egypt and then saves them at the Sea of Reeds. Where are the Israelites themselves in the story? Where is the human role in the bringing of redemption? What part of redemption is our responsibility? To answer those questions, the rabbis, as they often did, inserted a different story between the lines.

According to the rabbis' telling, Moses leads the people to the banks of the sea. Then they hear the hoofbeats of Pharaoh's approaching armies. The people cry out to Moses. Moses prays to God. He is told to hold his staff over the sea, an act that will cause the sea to split. And all that he does, exactly as he is commanded—but the sea doesn't split. He tries again, but the waters still do not part. He becomes nervous. He tries to recall the exact words of God, the exact instructions. Once again he holds the staff over the waters. And once again they do not part. Moses panics. The people panic. Everyone is immobilized with fear. And no one knows what to do.

No one, that is, except one man. One man perceived what even Moses Our Teacher could not. His name was Nachshon ben Aminadav, one of the princes of the tribes of Israel. Nachshon understood that God was waiting. God had sent Moses. And God had brought the plagues. And God had led the Israelites out of Egypt. But now God was waiting for the people to take a role in their own redemption. God, Nachshon understood, would not part the sea until someone moved—until someone moved toward his or her own redemption, until someone was ready to risk his or her life to bring about salvation.

And so Nachshon ben Aminadav jumped into the waters of the Red Sea.

At first everyone looked at him in wonder and awe. "What are you doing?" his family shouted. But he paid no heed; he knew exactly what he was doing. And he waded out farther, until water covered his knees. His family screamed and shouted and begged him to return, but he went farther still, until water reached his waist. And now everyone stood in silence and watched. He waded even farther, until water covered his shoulders. And then a few more steps—and he disappeared under the water. And only when the water had covered his nostrils and Nachshon could no longer breathe, only when he began to drown—only then did the sea split and the Israelites cross in safety.

For the rabbis of the Talmud, heaven and earth are not distinct. We human beings aren't just passive spectators to a divine drama. We are God's partners, sharing the work of bringing the world to perfection. God needs us. And every act made by a human being to advance the dream of a perfect world is a revelation of God's will in the world. In the poetic words of Abraham Joshua Heschel, "All of human history as described by the Bible may be summarized in one phrase: God in search of man."

- What's the difference between the way the Torah tells the story of the Red Sea and the way the Midrash tells it?

- What did Nachshon know that no one else knew?

- In our time, who are the Nachshons? Have you ever been a Nachshon?

Challahs in the Ark

Miracles happen all the time. Too often they go by unnoticed and unappreciated. What we lack is the vision to see them. We expect miracles to be momentous, history-shaping events that descend from heaven. But sometimes miracles are quiet, private moments when life is renewed and hope is rekindled.

Once, many years ago in a small village, there lived Reb Chaim, the richest man in the village, and Reb Yankel, the poorest. Every Friday evening, Reb Chaim would come to the synagogue in his fine *Shabbos* coat and his exquisite fur hat. He arrived early so that he could exchange greetings with all the other men of the village.

As the service ended, Red Chaim would rise, wish the congregation a good *Shabbos*, and then stride up the hill to his magnificent mansion. His butler met him at the door and showed him into his regal dining room, where a table fit for a king awaited him. Reb Chaim would sit surrounded by the very finest china, flatware, and crystal. He would be served the most remarkable *Shabbos* meal, accompanied by the sweetest, most heavenly challah. But none of it brought Reb Chaim joy. For he was alone. Reb Chaim had no family and no one he could call a friend.

One *Shabbos*, Reb Chaim stared at the golden platters and the wonderful dishes set before him, and he suddenly realized what he needed: He needed to share his *Shabbos* feast with someone. But with whom? "Who is worthy of sharing *Shabbos* feast?" he wondered. "Only God!" he decided. "Let God share my wonderful *Shabbos* feast!" A plan took shape in his mind.

"Bring me the baker!" Reb Chaim called out.

The baker emerged from the kitchen. "Yes, sir?" inquired the baker. "Is something wrong?"

"Wrong? No! Your challah is divine! Next week I would like you to make me two extra challahs. Make sure they're your very best! Pack them up for delivery before I leave for the synagogue."

"Yes, sir, my very best," replied the baker.

The next Friday evening, Reb Chaim left for the synagogue unusually early. He wore his *Shabbos* coat and his fur hat, and under his arm he carried a package still warm from the oven.

He entered the synagogue before anyone else and approached the Holy Ark. He stood for a moment in prayer: "Master of the Universe, each week I enjoy a magnificent *Shabbos* feast. This week I want You, God, to share my feast. I want Your *Shabbos* to be as good as mine. So I have brought You challahs. Even You, God, have never tasted challah so good! I hope You enjoy these challahs as I do! I wish You a good *Shabbos*!"

With that Reb Chaim opened the Ark, removed the challahs from the package, and tucked them behind the Torah scrolls. He closed the Ark, and as people began to enter the synagogue, he took his place by the eastern wall.

Reb Yankel also went to the synagogue that Friday night. But Reb Yankel, the poorest man in the village, always arrived late because he tried to squeeze every last bit of work into the waning minutes of every Friday afternoon. He always came to the synagogue in his dirty work clothes and always sat in the very back.

Normally Reb Yankel would hurry home after the service. He lived in a tiny hovel at the edge of the village with his wife, his children, his wife's parents, his wife's widowed sister, and assorted nieces and nephews, all of whom Yankel struggled to support. Normally he would enjoy the hugs and kisses of his family as he washed and readied himself for the *Shabbos* meal. No matter how meager the meal, Yankel cherished the spirit of his family's *Shabbos* table.

Tonight, however, Yankel was in no hurry. It had been a bad week, a bad month, a bad season. Each week, Yankel's family had

had less and less to eat. And tonight he could not bring himself to face his children over an empty table. So he sat in the synagogue as everyone left. And when he was alone, he approached the Holy Ark, stood a few minutes, and offered his prayer: "Master of the World, it's *Shabbos*! How can You let me go home to see my children hungry? You know how hard I work. And You know that I have nothing to bring home. Without Your help, dear God, I don't have the strength to go home and watch my family suffer! Without Your help, God, I refuse to leave the synagogue!" With that, he slammed his hands on the doors of the Holy Ark. The Ark opened up, and out rolled two beautiful, golden, warm challahs.

"It's a miracle!" shrieked Reb Yankel. "Thank You, dear God, thank You!"

Reb Yankel ran home and placed the challahs on the table. The family was astounded, and Yankel declared the challahs a gift, a miracle of God, an answer to his prayers. The family ate and celebrated.

It would be difficult to measure where there was greater joy that Friday night—in the tiny, poor home of Reb Yankel, whose children had never tasted challah so sweet, or in the mansion of Reb Chaim, who ate and drank and sang his prayers with a new spirit.

The following week, Reb Chaim again ordered his baker to make two challahs and pack them for delivery. And again Reb Chaim stood before the Holy Ark and offered his prayer: "Master of the World, You must have enjoyed those challahs because the next morning when we removed the Torah from the Ark, not a crumb was left! I'm grateful that Your *Shabbos* was as joyful as mine. And so I bring You two more challahs—challahs sweeter than those Your own angels bake. Enjoy these challahs, dear God, and I wish You a good *Shabbos*!"

At the end of the service, when the synagogue was empty, Reb Yankel humbly approached the Holy Ark. "Master of the World," he prayed, "I have come to give thanks for the joy You brought my family last week. I know that one miracle in a lifetime is more than a man has a right to ask for. And I know that I have no right to ask for another. But dear God, You Yourself heard our songs last week. You know what a *Shabbos* You brought my children. Besides, in Your great Universe, what's a couple of challahs?"

With that he timidly opened the Ark, and out rolled two more golden challahs. Yankel shouted in joy, "A miracle!" and he danced his way home.

This went on for a full month. And another. And another. Until a whole year of challahs had gone by. Each week, Reb Chaim placed his gifts for God in the Ark. And each week, Reb Yankel accepted God's miracles. It was the greatest year in each man's life.

Then a terrible thing happened. The *shammes*—the man who cleaned the synagogue—had been detained and so was late preparing for the Friday-night service. Just before the service was about to begin, he ran to the synagogue to do his weekly sweeping. As he worked in the back of the synagogue, he witnessed the strangest thing: Reb Chaim, the richest man in the village, approached the Holy Ark carrying a bundle. He made a quiet prayer and then opened the bundle and placed two challahs into the Ark.

The *shammes* wondered whom the challahs were for, so he waited to find out. Sure enough, as the service came to an end, Reb Yankel, the poorest man in the village, approached the Ark. He whispered a prayer about miracles and then opened the Ark and removed the challahs that Reb Chaim had placed there.

The *shammes* began to laugh, startling Reb Yankel. "You fool!" he declared. "You simpleton! Wait, stay right here." And with that the *shammes* ran outside, caught up with Reb Chaim, and dragged him back to the synagogue.

When the two men faced each other, their faces dropped. The *shammes* laughed as he ridiculed them both. "You, Reb Chaim, do you really think God eats your challah each week? You fool! It is this beggar who takes from you! And you, Reb Yankel, do you really believe that God hears your prayers and miraculously feeds your family? You fool! It is this miser! You are the most foolish men! Wait until the village hears of this!"

The spirits of both Reb Chaim and Reb Yankel shriveled. Reb Chaim trudged up the hill to his home but refused even to taste his *Shabbos* feast. And Reb Yankel dropped the challahs, walked home empty-handed, and sat weeping during the *Shabbos* meal.

Just as *Shabbos* ended, each of the three men—Reb Chaim, Reb Yankel, and the *shammes*—received an urgent message summoning them to the home of the rabbi. Now the rabbi was a great and powerful mystic with deep, penetrating eyes. And to receive a summons to his home filled the men with great fear.

The three were shown into the rabbi's room. The rabbi sat at his desk, staring into a holy book, shaking his head, and groaning in sadness. He looked up at the men, and they could see the anger and pain in his eyes. "I had a terrible dream last night," he began. "God was terribly angry and was ready to destroy the whole world because something precious and holy had been destroyed. So I pleaded with God to let me try to repair the miracle before the world was destroyed.

"Reb Chaim," the rabbi continued, "your gifts did reach God. And do you know what joy God took from them? And Reb Yankel, what you found each *Shabbos* did come from God. And do you know that your children's songs reached higher than the songs of the angels? Did you know that this miracle had been foreseen since the Creation of the world? It was God's special joy to see it renewed each week. And only if the miracle is repaired will God let the world continue to exist!"

Looking at each other for the first time, Reb Chaim and Reb Yankel knew what to do. The following Friday night, instead of opening the doors of the Ark to his challahs, Reb Chaim opened the doors of his home to the family of Reb Yankel, and in turn the children of Reb Yankel's family filled the rooms of Reb Chaim's once lonely and empty mansion with *Shabbos* song and spirit. And so because these two found the way to repair God's miracle, the world continues to exist.

As for the *shammes*, his punishment was to leave the village and spend the rest of his days wandering the earth. And in every place where he found Jews who make *Shabbos*, he told them the story of the miracle of Reb Chaim and Reb Yankel. When he died, his children continued to tell the story. And when they died, their children continued to tell the story, and so on until every Jew in every corner of the world had heard the story. In that way, the shammes repaired the miracle and helped the world continue.

And now you've heard the story, too.

When we enter a synagogue, we are drawn toward the Holy Ark. The Holy Ark is the focal point of the synagogue and its most holy place. In the Ark are the Torah scrolls, God's words and wisdom. But Torah isn't only a book. Torah is also a process of giving and taking. When we have wisdom and strength, we give. When we are in need, we take. Torah is a living connection among us. That's why the Torah is called eitz chaim, *a living tree, a tree of life, a source of nourishment and renewal.*

- Why was Reb Chaim so unhappy when he consumed his sumptuous Shabbat feast? What finally brought him happiness?

- What did Reb Yankel truly want from God?

- Why did the *shammes* embarrass the two men? Do you think his punishment fit his crime?

- Why did the rabbi believe that the fate of the whole world rested on this miracle?

Elijah's Stick

Each of us has a hero within. Each of us is capable of heroic acts, courageous acts, and acts of greatness. But sometimes we need a shove to inspire us to act heroically.

There was once a very old man who lived alone in a tiny cottage. The old man had no family and rarely any visitors. He was sustained only by his love for *Eiliyahu haNavi,* Elijah the Prophet. Elijah was his hero. The man knew every story and every legend about Elijah and recited them all with a twinkle in his eye. As he told each story, he would offer a prayer: "If only once in my life I could do something so wonderful." And then he would shrug his shoulders, cast his glance to the floor, and sigh, "But I am just an old fool filled with dreams."

Late one night as the old man dozed in front of his fire, a book of Elijah's tales on his lap, there came a knock at the door.

"Who comes so late at night?" he wondered. As he opened the door, he beheld a stranger—a tall man with a long, pointed beard. The stranger wore an odd cloak and a wide-brimmed hat and carried a walking stick.

"I am sorry to bother you," the stranger said in a strange accent, "but it seems I have lost my way in the dark and the cold. May I trouble you to spare me a place to rest until daybreak, when I can continue my journey?"

The old man stared in fascination and responded, "Of course, come in. Rest by the fire. Let me fix you some hot tea." And then he asked, "Where are you from?"

"From far away," the stranger responded.

"And where are you going?"

"A long, long way."

The old man nodded in acknowledgment and offered the stranger the cup of tea. The stranger expressed his appreciation for the tea and the fire and the chance to come in out of the cold. "Please, let me be no trouble," he said.

The two men stared into the fire and sipped their tea. Soon the old man dozed off. He dreamed of the stranger. And in his dream the stranger handed him his walking stick in appreciation for his hospitality.

"I can't accept such a gift!" the old man protested.

Said the stranger, "Then let it be a loan!"

"But how will I return it to you?" he asked.

"Don't worry. One day you will return it," the stranger replied.

When the old man awoke, it was morning, and the stranger was gone. As he ate his breakfast, he remembered the stranger, and he wondered if it had all been a dream. Then he saw that the stranger had indeed left his walking stick. "Perhaps he really was here!" exclaimed the old man. He lifted the stick. "A sunny day, a good stick—I think a walk into town is in order!" he thought cheerfully.

He set out on his walk, stick in hand. Walking with the stick renewed his strength. There was a new spring in his step, and he quickly arrived in town. There, standing on the corner of the busiest intersection, he saw an old blind woman crying for help.

"Help me across! Won't anyone help me across?"

The avenue was broad and busy with traffic, and there was no way she could have crossed alone. "I should help her," thought the old man. "That's certainly what Elijah would do! But I'm just an old man. We might both end up under the wheels of a wagon." He planned to sneak past the woman unnoticed.

Suddenly something strange happened. The walking stick began to shake. He held it tight and went where it went, and the stick shoved him into the old woman.

"Oh, oh, excuse me. I do apologize," he gasped.

"Please, just help me across the road," she replied.

"Of course," he said, staring at the stick in disbelief. He led her safely across the street, the stick in the lead.

"Thank you, young man," said the old lady.

"It was nothing," the old man replied, still bewildered.

That evening the entire town was invited to celebrate a wedding. The old man took his walking stick and joined the celebration. The square was lit up, and the air was filled with music. Everyone danced. The townsmen lifted the couple up on chairs as a band played happy wedding songs. The old man sat alone, watching the celebration and thinking, "If Elijah were here, he'd show them what real dancing looks like! But I am just an old man. It's best I get home."

He had taken only a few steps when the stick began to shake. "Oh, no, not again!" thought the man. The stick spun him around. He whirled about, this way and that, gripping the stick for dear life.

"Whoa! Whooooah!" he shouted. The dancers cheered the old man.

As the intensity of the music neared a climax, the stick flung the man high in the air. The dancers caught him. They held him aloft and carried him to the bride and groom, who hugged and kissed him and thanked him for his remarkable dance.

The old man was too winded to reply. "I think I will go home," he finally managed to gasp.

He took up his stick and began the walk home. As he trudged through the dark streets of the town, he passed an alleyway. He thought he heard a scream. He could see no more than a few feet into the alley. Then he was sure he heard a scream.

"Someone's in trouble," the old man thought. "But I'm just an old man. What can I do?"

He intended to continue on his way, but again the stick began to shake, and then it swung him around and pulled him into the alley. He saw a woman huddled over the body of a man. There were three robbers—huge men with sharp knives—taunting the woman.

"Please," she begged, "take what you will, but leave us in peace."

"We haven't finished our fun yet!" responded the leader as the other two laughed.

The robbers noticed the old man with the stick. "What do you want, old man?" one asked. "Get lost before we decide to have some fun with you too!"

"I think you should let these people be," the old man replied, mustering all his courage.

"Oh, yeah?" said one. The robbers forgot about the woman, turning their attention to the old man. They pointed their knives in his direction. "And what do you intend to do about it?" the leader asked.

The walking stick began to spin around, whooshing through the air like a propeller. The leader of the robbers advanced toward the old man. He wore a cruel smile and jabbed his knife in the air. "This should be fun!" he announced.

Just then the stick changed direction, catching the lead robber squarely on the chin. Before he could let out a shriek of surprise, the other end of the old man's stick had smashed him squarely in the back. He fell to his knees as the stick struck his wrist, sending his knife skidding through the alley.

The second robber lunged at the old man. "You think you're tough?" he taunted. The stick spun around again, smashing him in the kneecaps and clobbering him on the head. He, too, fell to the ground.

Seeing his partners dispatched, the third robber dropped his knife and ran into the night.

The old man fell to his knees and sighed in exhaustion.

"Thank you, sir. Thank you for saving our lives," cried the woman.

Her husband, now revived, asked, "How did you do that? Where did you learn to fight like that?"

"I don't know," said the old man. "I just wanted to help."

"You saved our lives. How can we ever repay you?"

"It was nothing. Please. I must be getting home."

The old man walked with the couple as far as the main street, and then they parted ways. He returned home, set the stick near the door, sat down in front of the fire, and fell fast asleep.

Early the next morning there came a loud knocking at his door. The old man stirred, dragged himself up, and answered the door. Before him stood a uniformed messenger, who informed him that the prince requested that he appear before him immediately. In all his life the old man had never gone near the palace. With not a little fear, the old man dressed and joined the messenger in the waiting carriage.

The carriage carried them up the hill and through the palace gates. A footman opened the door to the palace and escorted the old man into the library. There stood the prince and, alongside him, an older man and woman. It was the couple the old man had saved the night before.

"Is this the man?" the prince asked the couple. His voice was stern and commanding.

"Yes, that's him. He's the one."

The old man was afraid. Was he being accused? Had he done something wrong?

The prince turned to the old man. His voice became kind. "My dear sir, last night my aunt and uncle went for an evening walk. They were set upon by a band of robbers and surely would have been killed had you not come to their rescue. You saved their lives. And I am eternally grateful to you." With that the prince bowed deeply.

The old man was overwhelmed. "It was what anyone would have done," he said.

"Oh, no," the prince replied, "I'm told that you took on three armed bandits all by yourself, with only a walking stick as a weapon! It is my desire to reward you for your bravery and compassion. I am told by my contacts in the town that you have always wanted to visit Eretz Yisrael. A visit there shall be your reward. It is a gift from my family to express our gratitude."

The old man was speechless. Visit Eretz Yisrael? Walk where Elijah walked? It was almost more than he could grasp. "Thank you! Thank you, sir," he managed to say.

Soon thereafter the old man was on his way. He boarded a
ship bound for the Land of Israel. When he disembarked at the
port of Jaffa, he realized that he knew no one in the Land and
had no idea where he was going. But the walking stick led him. It
took him over the roads, across the hills, and through the valleys
of Eretz Yisrael. It guarded him as he slept and guided him as he
beheld the holy sites.

Then one day he arrived at the crest of Mount Carmel, where
Elijah had triumphed over the followers of the idol Ba'al. This
was the place that he had longed to see all his life. The day was
warm and lovely. The breezes filled the air with a wondrous
scent. The old man sat down on the hill, set down his walking
stick, and soon dozed off. He dreamed of the same stranger who
had come to his home that cold, cold night. "Thank you, old
friend, for returning my walking stick," said the stranger. "I hope
you enjoy this beautiful mountain as much as I do. May we share
many more dreams together."

The old man woke with a start and looked around him. The
stick was gone! And where the stick had been there grew a beautiful
tree, its boughs heavy with fruit and flowers.

The old man built a cottage under the branches of that tree
and lived there all the rest of his long life, sitting by the fire and
sharing stories of Elijah with his visitors.

According to the Bible, Elijah never died.

*According to the Book of Kings, he entered heaven on a fiery chariot.
According to folklore, Elijah still lives: He wanders the world performing
good deeds, making things right. And ultimately Elijah is the prophet who
will announce the Messiah and the Redemption of the world. This is why
Elijah visits every Passover seder, which is both a celebration of the past
and a rehearsal for the great Redemption of the future.*

In the household of Rav Naftali, the Ropshitzer rebbe, a wonderful custom was observed. The "cup of Elijah" stood empty on the seder table throughout the seder. But when it came time to welcome Elijah, the cup was passed from person to person, each contributing some of his or her own wine to Elijah's cup. In that way, everyone contributed his or her strength and vision to help Elijah bring Redemption.

- The old man always dreamed of doing heroic deeds as Elijah had done. What did it take to make his dream come true?

- Is there a hero inside all of us? How do you know? If there is, what does it take to bring it out and make it real?

- Have you ever met a true hero? What made him or her a hero?

The Maccabees' Sister

There are certain people who see the world through God's eyes. They feel God's pain and distress, and they call upon the rest of us to help God make the world right. We call such people prophets or sages or seers. Sometimes they are celebrated as heroes. Sometimes they are never recognized for the work they do to change the world.

We know of great Mattathias and his brave sons, the Maccabees: Judah, Eliezer, Simon, Yochanan, and Yonatan. We know that they fought the Greeks, liberated the Holy Temple from idolatry, and returned Israel to the worship of God. We know the story of the lights, the miracle of the menorah, in which one tiny jar of oil burned for eight nights, demonstrating that God had returned to the midst of the Jewish people. We know that the Maccabees minted coins and celebrated God's miracles in rescuing the Jews.

But we forget that the Maccabees had a sister. Her name was Dinah. And it was because of her that all those miracles came to be. Dinah is the real hero of the Hanukkah story. So let's remember how it happened.

When Antiochus and the rest of the Greeks brought idols into the Holy Temple in Jerusalem, the Jews did not protest. There was a harvest to bring in, crops to store before the winter. Everyone was too busy to protest.

When the Greeks made the Jews of Jerusalem bow down and worship the idols and forced them to abandon their study of Torah, the rites of the Covenant, the worship of God, no one said a thing. There were families to raise, children to teach, elders to care for, homes to tend. Who had time for politics?

When the Greeks brought their idols to the towns of Judah and forced Jews to abandon the God of their ancestors and bow low to Zeus, no one stood up and protested. Who needed the trouble? Who wanted to face down armed soldiers? After all, they were only farmers. "Better to keep quiet," they thought, "lay low, attract no attention, in the hope that the Greeks will go away." But the Greeks didn't go away. Instead, Antiochus and the Greeks pushed forward through the towns and villages of Judah, destroying the faith of Israel. And still no one did anything.

Once the harvest was in, it was time for the village feasts. The farmers and their families gathered to celebrate the bounty of the land and the blessings of God. In the town of Modi'in, the town of Mattathias and his family, Jewish farmers and craftsmen, shop-keepers and laborers, came together for a night of celebration. With singing and dancing and feasting, they gave thanks for all that God had given them. The presence of Antiochus and his armies in the land was soon forgotten. Thoughts of the desecration of the Holy Temple were replaced by the pleasures of the joyful feast.

Only Dinah remembered. Only Dinah could feel the shame of the Holy Temple as if it were in her own body. And she could feel the evil of Antiochus that crept upon the Land of Israel as if it crept along her own arms and legs. Why could no one else feel it? Why did no one else care?

She cried out to her brothers, "Jerusalem has been ruined, and our Temple has been wrecked! Why don't you do something?"

They laughed at her. "Little sister, what could we do? We are farmers; they are soldiers. Besides, tonight is the feast. All year we have waited for the feast!"

"How can you feast? How can you celebrate? Can't you feel the evil that has come upon our land?" she inquired.

Again they laughed at her. "Little sister, you sound like a prophet! Go and play with the girls, and let us enjoy our feast!"

But Dinah did not give up. She faced her brothers and pleaded: "Judah, you are the bravest. Are you afraid to fight these Greeks? Eliezer, no man is mightier than you. Why are you suddenly so weak? Simon, you are the wisest of us. Can you not see what is coming this way? Yochanan, Yonatan, you are the most loyal and the most loving. Where is your faithfulness?"

"Little sister, enough of your nonsense!" they answered. "Let us go and enjoy our feast, and stop pestering us with your whining! Go dress for the feast! Buy yourself a new outfit!"

But Dinah couldn't forget. Nothing could distract her from the troubles of her people, her land, her holy city and its Temple. But how could she arouse her brothers? How could she persuade them to rise up and fight? She was, after all, only a girl.

That night the great feast began. The whole town gathered in the square to eat and drink and dance in joyful celebration. Music filled the air, along with the sounds of song and laughter. The whole town danced in the square. It was late in the evening, in the midst of all the celebration, when a mysterious woman came up onto the stage where the musicians played. She was swathed in beautiful veils, only her eyes revealed. She beckoned the musicians to play, and she began an alluring dance. All the town stopped to watch her. And everyone gasped when, with one graceful flick of the wrist, she removed a veil and revealed a trace of skin. Now everyone was watching intently. Another flick of the wrist and another veil disappeared. The music played faster and faster; the dancer whirled. Another flick and another veil melted away—and another and yet another. The crowd cheered and screamed. The dancer's face was still covered, but not much else, as each veil floated off the body of the beautiful dancer.

"Who is she?" people whispered. "Who is this mysterious dancer?"

As the music came to its wild climax, the dancer whirled about, covered only by one translucent veil. The music stopped, and she flung back her long hair. The veil on her face dropped away, and everyone could see—it was Dinah.

Her five brothers bolted toward the stage. They grabbed her, wrapped her in a blanket, and began to pull her away.

"No!" Dinah screamed. "Don't touch me!"

"But you are nearly naked!" the brothers shouted. "Here, in front of our neighbors and friends, you stand with almost nothing on! Have you no shame? Are you not embarrassed? What have you done to our family's honor?"

Dinah straightened up and looked directly into the eyes of her big brother Judah. "Am I embarrassed, dear brother? Am I shamed because I stand in the square of our town before our neighbors with no clothes, with nothing to protect me? Tonight our Holy Temple stands naked in the world with no one to protect her, with no one to rise up and defend her honor. Tonight our holy city stands shamed and defiled, and no one runs to her side. Tonight the living God is taken from the people Israel, and no one rises to stand with God. No, brother, I am not ashamed. But you? Have you no shame? Are you not embarrassed? What has happened to the honor of Israel?"

Judah and his brothers looked at their sister, and then they looked at one another. Each man knew that his sister was right. The time had come to defend the honor of Israel and the Presence of God.

Judah drew his sword and proclaimed, "Whoever is for God, come with me!"

And thus began the miracle of Hanukkah that we all know. Mattathias, Judah, Eliezer, Simon, Yochanan, and Yonatan were all heroes. But the hero who inspired them to fight for God and Israel was their sister, Dinah.

"Our rabbis taught, 'When... [the Maccabees] prevailed against and defeated... [the Greeks], they made search and found only one cruse of oil. ... Then a miracle occurred and the lamp burned for eight days.'"
—Talmud Shabbat 21b

When the world was plunged into darkness, all it took was one tiny light. When the world was filled with fear and despair, all it took was one tiny spark of courage and hope. When the Torah was taken from the Jewish people, all it took was one loyal family. It has always been this way. Light, hope, courage, loyalty, always begin with one special soul.

- The Maccabees were heroes. How is Dinah a hero as well? What was she willing to sacrifice to save the Jewish people?

- Hanukkah is about lighting lights on the darkest nights of the year. What light did Dinah light when the world was dark?

The Cursed Harvest

Have you ever looked at the world around you, watched the news, or listened to the radio and wondered if the whole society had gone mad? What if such worldwide madness did exist?

There was once a king who ruled his kingdom with justice and wisdom. The goodness and fairness of the king offended those who wished to do evil. Included in this number was a wizard. The wizard hated the king, and he hated the integrity with which the king ruled. The wizard devised a plan to destroy the king, the kingdom, and all who were dear to the king. He cursed the harvest. Anyone who ate of the harvest for seven years would be driven insane.

In the court of the king, there was a prophet. This prophet learned of the wizard's curse—not in time to stop him, but in time to offer the king a warning. As the harvest was being brought in, the prophet brought the news to the king: "Anyone who eats of this harvest for the next seven years will turn mad."

The king was distressed. What could be done? How could he save his people? He ordered that all the uncontaminated food-stuffs of the kingdom be gathered and measured. He gathered his circle of advisers to ask their advice: "What can we do to protect the kingdom from this curse?"

It was determined that there was just enough food to sustain one person for the seven years of the curse. Only one person could eat of the uncontaminated food and remain sane and sober while the rest of the kingdom sank into madness. But who?

Whom would the king trust with this impossible mission? And what could one sane person do in a kingdom of the mad?

The king turned to his trusted friend the prophet. "You shall be the one," he charged. "You shall be given the uncontaminated food, enough for the seven years of the curse. You shall eat. And while all the rest of us sink into madness, you shall be the one who remains sane, sober, and rational."

"But, Your Majesty, what can one man do? What can one sane man do in a kingdom of the mad?"

The king replied, "You cannot keep us from our madness, but you must remind us that we are mad. Ride through the kingdom, and proclaim aloud, 'My brothers and sisters, remember the curse. Remember you are mad!'"

It was a daunting and lonely responsibility. But the prophet so loved the king he accepted the task. And so it came to be that all in the kingdom ate of the cursed harvest. And all of them became insane. In their speech and dress and behavior, they were quite mad. It was the daily task of the loyal prophet to ride through the kingdom as he had been charged, proclaiming: "My brothers and sisters, remember the curse! Remember that you are mad!"

One day during the years of the curse, as he rode about the kingdom proclaiming his truth, one of the citizens of the kingdom looked up at him with curiosity. "If it is true, my brother, that we are mad because of the curse and you are the only sane one among us, why do you proclaim it? What good will it do?" he asked. "If we are mad, how will your proclamation change anything? Isn't this your own madness?"

A thoughtful question from a madman, thought the prophet. Indeed, what good does it do? Was this task just his own madness? Had the curse affected him as well?

He declared: "I proclaim this truth out of loyalty to my king, who charged me to do so. I proclaim this so that you might stop a moment before you act and perhaps wonder if your act derives not from any reason but from the curse's madness. You may be mad, but perhaps this once you will not choose to behave in the way of the insane. Perhaps this once you will choose the alternative and behave in a manner that is reasoned, just, and wise."

And then the prophet sighed, thinking of all the mad behavior he had witnessed these many years. He thought of all the senseless brutality, the mindless cruelty, the self-destructive acts he had witnessed. He realized that his aspiration was probably a vain hope. Perhaps the madman was right. Perhaps he was as mad as the rest.

Then he thought again and he declared: "No, if nothing else succeeds, this I know. By fulfilling my charge, by never ceasing to proclaim your insanity, by warning you and begging you to behave in a manner more reasoned and more humane, this I am certain I shall achieve: I shall remain sane. More than the food I eat, this is my way to remain sane and sensible."

"Very well, my brother," replied the thoughtful madman, "fulfill your charge and offer your proclamation. Perhaps one day soon we will awaken from this curse and join you on your mission!"

In a world gone mad, how does the sane person keep his or her senses? How does he or she keep from being seduced or coerced into accepting or accommodating the world's insanity? Answering these questions is one of the functions of Torah. Torah is a counterculture, an alternative sensibility, enabling us to step back and question the world about us. Prayer, study, and mitzvot *offer us access to a different view of the world with a different sense of what's right, true, and beautiful.*

- What's insane in our world?

- How can a sane person keep his or her sanity in a world gone mad?

- Do you think the crazy people in the kingdom ever tired of hearing the prophet's proclamation? How might they have reacted to it?

The Holy Thief

The Hasidic master Rabbi Levi Yitzchak of Berdichev loved all Jews. He even loved the scoundrels and thieves among the Jewish people, believing that everyone carries some spark of divine light. Everyone has a role to play in God's world. This is one of Rabbi Yitzchak's great stories.

In the Jewish villages of eastern Europe, there lived a notorious thief. The Jews of those villages were very poor, but what little they had he managed to steal from them. Some days it was a purse of coins mistakenly left on a store counter. Other days it was a cloak or a pair of boots set aside while its owner enjoyed an afternoon nap. On rare occasions something valuable—a silver Kiddush cup or even a horse—might find its way into his possession. And of course every Friday he stole two challahs and a flask of wine so that he and his family might enjoy a Sabbath feast as all Jews do.

He was reviled. But with characteristic Jewish love, he was accepted as a member of the community. Thievery was simply his way of making a living. And as occupations go, it was not all that much more dishonest and sinful than many other occupations. The town butcher, for example, was known to have scales that were accurate, but only within a pound or two.

The thief was effective at what he did, but he pursued his trade according to a distinct code of ethics: He never stole from the very poor. He never stole anything that was essential to its owner's life or livelihood. He never took anyone's last ruble. And he stole only to support himself and his family.

When the thief's days were finished, his soul ascended to Heaven to stand before Judgment. Heaven was not eager to accept him, not because his evil was so heinous but simply because the residents of Heaven did not look forward to finding their possessions pinched. So he was sent to Hell for an indeterminate sentence.

In Hell the thief was welcomed as a celebrity. No mere clerk would be assigned his file for processing. Instead, the very Prince of Darkness, the Unholy One, the Master of Hell himself would handle his case. And so the thief was shown into the offices of the master.

Running Hell in our time is no small task. The master was terribly busy. He gestured to the thief to have a seat while he attended to some pressing business. When the business was concluded, the master turned and welcomed his new guest warmly. He described with relish how he and all his associates in Hell had followed and celebrated the thief's lifetime of exploits and how honored they were to have him among them.

During their conversation the Master of Hell revealed to the thief his pride and joy: a giant folio book, which sat upon his ornate desk. For generations and generations, he explained, he had been carefully building a case against the people Israel. He would soon bring this case before Heaven's court. In that giant book he had carefully recorded every sin committed by every Jew in every way. All the unkosher food, broken promises, Sabbaths desecrated, all the curses uttered quietly and aloud, all the charity monies slipped quietly into a pocket—all were meticulously inscribed in that huge book. The case was airtight. With all that evidence of sin and corruption, Heaven would be forced at last to grant him his fondest dream: the ultimate destruction of the Jewish people. Then, with the Jews gone, Hell would have no opposition on earth. There would be no one to thwart the master's plan to dominate humanity and fill the earth with evil. This evil dream was about to be realized. With glee the master revealed all this to the thief. All the evidence recorded in that huge folio was ready for presentation to the heavenly court.

As the master was concluding his speech, a messenger arrived with more pressing business. The master was distracted for but a moment as he turned to speak to the messenger.

The thief looked at the huge volume on the master's elegant desk. It would soon be presented to the heavenly court, and Hell would rain down on the people Israel and the world. The thief realized that it was for this very moment that he had been created. With exquisite clarity he realized what he had to do.

With hands trained over a lifetime of thievery, he deftly lifted the great book from under the elbow of the master himself. He lifted the book stealthily, and in one polished, practiced motion he carried it to the window overlooking the raging fires of Hell. It took but a split second for him to open the window and silently cast the giant book down, deep into the fires of Hell, where it was consumed instantaneously.

With the sudden rush of heat, the master turned from the messenger to see what had happened. He caught just a glimpse of his book dropping from the window and into the fires.

"No!" he screamed with unholy rage. "No! For generations I have toiled to bring Israel to destruction. And now you would rob me of my victory? No!" The master reached for the soul of the trembling thief and began to squeeze out its life. "You think you can rob from the source of all larceny? Do you know from whom you have robbed tonight?" he screamed into the suffocating soul of the hapless thief.

Suddenly the office filled with light. Two messengers from Heaven appeared before the Master of Hell.

"Cease!" they commanded. "We have a writ from on high. The soul of the thief is ours. Cease and desist!"

For just a moment the master hesitated. Then he relinquished the panting soul of the thief. "Very well," he said. "We just begin again. Soon enough I will fill another book with their sins."

The two messengers carried the startled soul of the thief toward Heaven, where it found repose for eternity as a reward for its courage in saving Israel and the world from the clutches of the Master of Darkness.

But every now and again, just to stay in practice, the holy thief sneaks out of Heaven. Secretly he sneaks down into the realm of the evil Master of Hell and steals a soul or two and brings them up into Heaven.

"There is no person who doesn't have his moment,
And there is no thing that doesn't have its place."
—Pirkei Avot 4:3

Nothing in God's Creation is wasted. Everything has a purpose. There is even a purpose for a thief. It just might take a moment to find it.

A rabbi was once asked by his students, "Is there a purpose for atheism, for doubt?" The rabbi responded, "Of course. Even atheism has a purpose. When a beggar comes to you in need of food, pretend there is no God to feed that hungry person and you are his only hope. Imagine that it is up to you to save that man's life."

- This was no ordinary thief. He was a thief with a conscience. How can you tell?

- At his moment of truth, the thief realized he could do something that perhaps no one else could do. What do you suppose went through his mind at that moment?

- Have you ever had the sense that a moment called upon you to do something only you could do? What was this moment like?

PART FOUR

Teachers and Friends

Get yourself a teacher, find yourself a friend.

(Pirkei Avot 1:6)

Rabbi Yochanan ben Zakai asked his students:
"What does a person need most for a good life?"
Rabbi Joshua answered: "A good friend."

(Pirkei Avot 2:13)

Capturing the Moon

The town of Chelm is the legendary home of the world's wisest fools or the world's most foolish wise people—no one is really sure which. They have a special way of solving problems in Chelm. If only the rest of the world were as wise as Chelm.

Of all things the people of Chelm loved, they loved the moon most of all. When it shone brightly in the night sky, there was joy and celebration in the town. Everything in the town was brighter: Homes would glow with happiness; lovers would walk through the town slowly, staring into each other's eyes; children would listen to their parents and their teachers; the old, the young, even dogs and cats were kind and considerate to one another. But when the moon waned and disappeared, a gloomy sadness settled over everyone.

"We have to do something about this!" proclaimed the town leaders. "We have to find a way to stay joyful even on the dark nights. But how?"

"If only we could capture the moon!" one Chelm genius declared. "Then we could let out a little light on those dark, gloomy nights and bring happiness to the world!"

"But how do you capture the moon?" the townspeople wondered.

"Well," offered Shmerel the tailor, "once I was eating a bowl of soup. And as I ate, I looked into the bowl. And in the bowl was the light of the moon. If we had a big enough bowl of soup, perhaps we could capture the moon!"

And so it was determined: They would build the world's biggest bowl, fill it with soup, and capture the moon!

In the town square a giant bowl was constructed. And one night as the moon shone brightly in the sky, the whole town came forth with soup—jars of soup, pots of soup, vats of soup, bathtubs full of soup. Soon they had filled the world's largest bowl. As the bowl filled up, the moon's brilliant light was reflected in it.

"There it is!" they shouted.

Stealthily they snuck up on the moon. Then, all at once, they slammed the top on the bowl. At that very moment a cloud covered the sky, blotting out the moon's light.

"We own the moon!" they shouted. "It is right here in the world's biggest bowl of soup. We own the moon!"

That night there was dancing and rejoicing all night long in the town of Chelm. But the next night, as the sun went down and darkness covered the land, the moon rose again, bright as ever, shining high in the sky.

Everyone in Chelm was perplexed. "How can the moon be in the sky? We captured it right here in the town square, in the world's biggest bowl of soup!"

"Someone must have let it out!" shouted Shoshanah the matchmaker.

"But who? Who would do such a terrible thing?" asked Avrum the butcher.

And so an investigation was launched. Everyone in the town was interrogated. Each person was required to account for his or her whereabouts all during the day. No one was spared. No one except, of course, the rabbi. No one suspected that the rabbi, beloved, wise, and learned, would…No—it couldn't be, not the rabbi!

But the investigation came up empty. Everyone had an alibi. Everyone was in school, at work, in the fields, in the shops, at home—everyone but the rabbi.

And so the townspeople of Chelm timidly approached their beloved rabbi.

"Learned Rabbi, did you let the moon out of the soup?" the designated spokesperson inquired.

"Yes," he sighed. "It was I."

A shock ran through the town.

"But why, dear Rabbi, why?" they persisted.

"Why?" He looked at them through his bushy white eyebrows and stroked his long white beard. "Why? Because there are things we enjoy while we have them. They are ours to own and to hold and to enjoy—"

"Like a shirt," someone offered, "or a shoe—"

"And there are other things," the rabbi continued, "things of far greater value, that we enjoy only when we share them. Do you know what things I mean?"

"Love?" someone suggested.

"Yes, love," he answered.

"And hugs!" someone else offered.

"Yes, hugs," he answered.

"And joy!" they shouted.

"Yes, joy," he responded.

"And the moon!" said Shmerel the tailor sadly.

"Yes, the moon as well," the rabbi responded. "Only when we share it can we really enjoy its light. And so I was the one who let the moon out. And now all the world can share it!"

"But what will we do now, on dark nights, when the moon disappears? We'll be sad and gloomy and dark," the people cried.

"That's true," responded the rabbi. "Into every life come times of sadness, darkness, and gloom. That's part of life. We'll just have to find something else to share that sustains us when that happens!"

"Like what?" they asked.

"Like soup!" declared the rabbi. "We'll share soup. If you can't own the moon and share happiness all the time, the next best thing is to share soup."

And so it was declared a tradition. On nights when the moon disappeared and the night sky grew dark and gloomy, everyone shared soup. And it helped. For soup may not bring happiness— but it helps.

*"For everything there is a season, and
a time for every purpose under heaven.
A time to be born and a time to die...
A time to weep and a time to laugh,
A time to mourn and a time to dance."*
—Ecclesiastes 3:1, 2, 4

*Understanding that there is no life that is all light and no darkness, all
joy and no pain, all celebration and no sadness, is the wisdom of Chelm.
The waxing and waning of the soul is part of the rhythm of life, just as
the waxing and waning of the moon is part of the rhythm of the world.
But a community of friends who share all life's celebrations and tears
gives us the strength to get through the dark nights as we anticipate the
return of the light. And having plenty of soup helps too.*

- Why did the rabbi convince the people that he had released the moon? Was he right to do so? Why or why not?

- Can we have a life filled only with light and joy, with no darkness and no sadness? What happens to people who expect that life will always be that way?

- What can we do to help ourselves through the sad and tough moments of life—besides eating borscht?

The Sukkah of Rabbi Pinchas

Ever get tired of the phone ringing, friends asking for just a little of your time, family members making ceaseless demands? Ever wish they would all go away and leave you alone? And if they did, how long would it be before you missed them? How long before you would discover that the greatest joy in life is knowing that you're needed and loved?

Everyone loved Rabbi Pinchas. Wherever he went, he was surrounded. As he walked briskly to the synagogue early on Shabbat, his students would catch up to him to try to acquire a morsel of learning. As he sat in the synagogue praying, children would come and sit on his lap. When he rose to teach, the synagogue was packed. And when he went home, a dozen women with a dozen kugels were waiting for him.

"Taste this kugel, Rabbi, and give me your blessing!"

What could he do? He carefully tasted all twelve kugels, savoring the love baked into each one. Then joyfully he pronounced twelve blessings: "May your life and the lives of your children be as sweet as this wonderful kugel!"

On holidays even more people came, especially on Sukkot. Sukkot is called *Z'man Simchateinu*, the Season of Our Joy. And no one's sukkah was more filled with joy than the sukkah of Rabbi Pinchas. His students filled the sukkah with learning. The community brought delicacies and treats for the feast. And children filled his sukkah with laughter and song. It was said, "If you haven't celebrated in the sukkah of Rabbi Pinchas, you don't know true joy!"

But despite all that love, Rabbi Pinchas was bothered. He knew that a great rabbi must write a great book. Only if he wrote a great book would he be remembered as a great rabbi long after he was gone. Rashi wrote great books. The Rambam did too. To be great, Rabbi Pinchas knew, he needed to write his own great book.

But how? He had no time to sit and write his great book. He was always taking care of someone, answering someone's question, offering someone a blessing. He was always being the rabbi. When could he sit alone and write his great book?

As time went on, this problem nagged Rabbi Pinchas.

So one Yom Kippur, Rabbi Pinchas prayed a strange prayer: "Take all these people away from me! Day and night they pester me. Day and night I listen to their needs. Give me quiet! Give me peace to sit and write my book! Let no one bother me!"

God heard the strange prayer and asked Rabbi Pinchas, "Is that what you really want? To be alone?"

"Yes!" responded Rabbi Pinchas. "Let me be in peace to write my book!"

"Very well," God answered. "Your prayer is fulfilled."

When Yom Kippur was over and the shofar had sounded, no one invited Rabbi Pinchas to break the fast. There were no crowds of people, no platters of food, no plates of sweets and treats to fill Rabbi Pinchas's home after Yom Kippur. Instead, Rabbi Pinchas walked home alone, sat in his home alone, broke his Yom Kippur fast with a piece of dry bread, and wrote the first page of his great book.

The next morning the townspeople were busy putting up their *sukkahs* for the coming holiday. Rabbi Pinchas waited for the men of the town to come with their tools and put up his sukkah. But no one came. So late in the afternoon he tried to erect the sukkah himself. He smashed his fingers hammering in the nails, dropped a heavy board on his toe, stuck himself with a thorn when he lifted the *s'chach,* the leaves for the sukkah's roof, and hurt his back dragging his table into the sukkah. But eventually his sukkah was finished. It was crooked. It was ugly. But it was finished.

For the next three days, Rabbi Pinchas wrote and rewrote the first page of his great book. Just as he had requested of God, he was alone. No one bothered him. Soon his house was so quiet he couldn't stand it. He went out for a walk. No one said hello. No one stopped to ask him a question. No one asked for a blessing. No one asked for his help. No one.

The first night of Sukkot arrived, and Rabbi Pinchas sat in his sukkah alone. No one came to celebrate. No one brought treats. No children, no laughter, no song. It was too quiet. Rabbi Pinchas ran out to the street. He went looking for someone, anyone to share his sukkah. But no one would come.

"How can I sit in a sukkah alone? What kind of festival is that?" Rabbi Pinchas asked himself. So he prayed the mystical *Ushpizin* prayer inviting his holy ancestors to share his sukkah: "May our father Abraham come and share my sukkah!"

Miraculously, the shining presence of Abraham appeared. But he would not enter Rabbi Pinchas's sukkah. He stood outside, near the door.

So Rabbi Pinchas prayed again: "May our father Isaac come and share my sukkah!"

And the shining presence of Isaac came. But he, too, stood outside.

Rabbi Pinchas prayed for our father Jacob, for Moses and Aaron, for King David and King Solomon. And miraculously they all appeared, their mystical light filling the yard. But they would not enter Rabbi Pinchas's sukkah. They stood outside.

Rabbi Pinchas was desperate. The loneliness was driving him mad. So he prayed one more time. He asked God to visit his sukkah.

God responded to the prayer of Rabbi Pinchas: "Where my children are not welcome, I am not welcome."

Rabbi Pinchas began to cry. He threw himself down on the ground and wept and prayed aloud: "I am sorry. I have made a terrible mistake. Bring me back my people. Bring me back my friends. Let them come and fill my life again. Please accept my prayer."

God heard the strange prayer and asked Rabbi Pinchas, "Is that what you really want? You know they will bother you until the day you die, and you may never write your book."

"Yes!" responded Rabbi Pinchas. "Let them come and bother me and pester me all they'd like! Let them come and fill my life with all their needs! They are my blessing! Just bring them back to me. I need them. I need them so badly."

"Very well," God answered. "Your prayer is fulfilled."

Before Rabbi Pinchas could even pick himself up, there was knocking at the door. The whole town had come to Rabbi Pinchas's sukkah. The townspeople came and fixed up his crooked, ugly sukkah. They brought platters and plates of treats for the feast. They brought learning. They brought questions. They brought laughter and song. They brought life.

And Rabbi Pinchas enjoyed every minute. Every question, every request for a prayer or a blessing, every child's song, brought him joy. He enjoyed that Sukkot holiday more than all the others put together. And the next year he enjoyed Sukkot even more.

Except for that very first page, Rabbi Pinchas never did write his great book. But he is remembered forever for his joy. They still say, "If you haven't celebrated in the sukkah of Rabbi Pinchas, you don't know true joy!"

"One who is beloved by others is beloved by God.
One who is reviled by others is reviled by God."
—Pirkei Avot 3:13

Jewish life is lived in community. The solitude of the monastery is not the way we find God. Rather, as the philosopher Martin Buber taught, we find God in moments of friendship, solidarity, and intimacy: "Behind every You stands the Eternal You." But community life can be unnerving, and relationships can be distracting. Sometimes we need to step back to refocus our vision and remember the blessings that come by means of the people we love.

- Why did Abraham, Isaac, Jacob, and the others refuse to enter Rabbi Pinchas's sukkah? Why didn't God enter?

- Why, do you suppose, did God grant Rabbi Pinchas's prayer to begin with? What did Rabbi Pinchas learn from his experience?

- Who are the people in your life (or your sukkah) who are your blessings?

Akiva and Rachel

We Jewish people have an odd way of showing people we love them: We send them to school. If you're in school, chances are someone loves you. Why school? In school we learn to become the people God wants us to be. School is a magical place—a place of love.

The wealthiest man in ancient Israel was ben Kalba Savu'a. He owned vast parcels of lands, farms, estates, and flocks and herds of animals. Ben Kalba Savu'a had a beautiful daughter, Rachel. It was his dream that his daughter would one day marry a great scholar. With a great scholar as his son-in-law, ben Kalba Savu'a would then have everything he wanted in life.

But Rachel had other ideas. Rachel fell in love with an illiterate shepherd, Akiva. She knew that something about Akiva was special. So even though her father objected, every day she would pack a picnic lunch and sneak out into the hills to meet Akiva.

Rachel lay her head on Akiva's lap. He stroked her long, beautiful hair. He gazed lovingly into her eyes and asked, "Rachel, will you marry me?"

"Akiva, I will marry you, but only if you make me a promise."

"Anything! I'll promise you anything!"

Rachel stood and looked directly into Akiva's eyes. "Promise me this, Akiva: When we are blessed with a child, you will go to school with our child and learn Torah."

"But Rachel, I'm an adult! I can't go back to school!" Akiva protested.

"Akiva, do you love me?" she asked as she touched his cheek with her fingers.

"Do I love you? I love you with all my heart!" he responded.

"Then promise me you'll go to school," she demanded.

"I promise," he answered.

And so they were married in secret.

When ben Kalba Savu'a found out that his beautiful daughter had married an illiterate shepherd, he was furious. He sent her from his house with nothing but the clothes she wore and vowed that she and her illiterate husband would never be welcome in his home.

Akiva and Rachel lived in a barn. They had few possessions, but their love was fierce, and God soon blessed them with a son.

When the son was three years old and ready for school, Rachel reminded Akiva of his promise: "You remember, Akiva, you promised me—when our child goes to learn Torah, you must go too!"

Akiva had hoped his wife might forget that promise. He couldn't see himself going to school as an adult. "But, Rachel, I'm too old. How can I go to school?" he complained.

"Akiva, do you love me?" she asked as she touched his cheek with her fingers.

"I love you with all my heart, dear Rachel!" he answered.

"Then go to school!"

She would not change her mind.

So he went, together with his three-year-old son. He sat at a tiny table on a tiny chair in the class of the three-year-olds. On his first day he learned the first two letters, *alef* and *bet*.

"I've fulfilled my promise!" he announced to Rachel. "I went to school and learned two letters, *alef* and *bet*."

"Now you'll go back and learn the rest of the letters!" she insisted.

"The rest of the letters? But, Rachel, I'm too old. I can't learn, not at my age!" he grumbled.

She wouldn't let him renege on his promise.

So off to school he went for the rest of the week. And he learned all the letters.

"Now I've learned all the letters. Now I've fulfilled my promise," Akiva proclaimed. "No more school!"

But Rachel knew better and sent him back to school again. He stayed for most of the year. He learned to read. And he began learning Torah. First Leviticus. And then the other books of the Torah.

When the year of school ended, he returned home and announced, "I have fulfilled my promise! I have learned Torah! That's all the school I need!"

Rachel looked deep into his eyes. "Akiva, do you love me?" she asked, touching his cheek with her fingers.

"Dear Rachel, I have missed you so this year. I love you with all my heart."

"Then go back and learn the rest. And don't come home until you're finished."

He knew she meant it. So he went back and studied for seven years. He returned home a scholar of Torah. But she was unsatisfied. Rachel wanted Akiva to pursue his learning even further, and so he returned to school for another seven years. During those years he became the great Rabbi Akiva.

Rabbi Akiva would visit all the towns and villages in the Land of Israel, teaching Torah. Everywhere he went, thousands of students followed him. One day he came to his own town, where Rachel lived. The whole town came to see the great rabbi. One by one, the people came before him to present gifts and to ask for his blessing.

There appeared before Rabbi Akiva a very poor woman. Out of respect, she lowered her eyes, never looking into his face. She did not recognize her beloved. She brought him only a small challah as a gift.

"Why such a small gift?" the rabbi asked.

"Many years ago I sent my husband to learn with the great rabbis. In his absence I have been very poor and shall continue to be until he returns."

"You sent your husband away to learn? Why would you do such a thing?" he asked.

"Because the first day I met him, I knew he was destined to be a great master of Torah. I saw that in his soul. I knew that it was my responsibility to make sure he would go and learn. Great Rabbi, I only pray that he will find in his own soul what I saw those many years ago."

Akiva's eyes filled with tears, and his heart filled with a greater love than he had ever known. He reached out and touched her cheek. "Rachel, do you love me?" he asked.

For the first time, she looked up and saw the face of her Akiva, and she, too, began to cry. "With all my heart, dear Akiva!" she answered.

Rabbi Akiva's students didn't understand who the woman was, so they tried to move her away from him, but he waved his hand and stopped them. "Let her be! All that I know and all I have taught you belong to her!"

Just then came the wealthiest man in the town, ben Kalba Savu'a. His gift to the rabbi was a golden jeweled tiara.

"Why do you bring such a magnificent gift to the rabbi?" Akiva asked him.

"Because my heart is broken, and I seek the rabbi's blessing," replied ben Kalba Savu'a. "Years ago I made a foolish vow. In anger I sent away my beautiful daughter because I objected to the man she married. And in anger I vowed that she and her illiterate husband would never have a place in my home. Every day since then I have regretted that vow. Every day I think of my daughter and miss her terribly. Every day I wish I could reach out and bring her home."

"And the husband? Why were you so angry with her husband?" Akiva inquired.

"I wanted her to marry a scholar, a man worthy of her," replied ben Kalba Savu'a.

"If you knew that today the man she married is a scholar, would you still reject him as unworthy?" Akiva asked.

"The man she married was an illiterate shepherd," ben Kalba Savu'a answered.

"Ben Kalba Savu'a," Akiva announced, "the man your daughter married stands before you! Your vow is released. Now go and bring your daughter home!"

Rabbi Akiva accepted the gift of the jeweled tiara from ben Kalba Savu'a and with it crowned his beloved Rachel. Ben Kalba Savu'a welcomed his daughter and son-in-law into his home. And because of Rachel's love, Rabbi Akiva became the greatest of the rabbis, just as Rachel knew he would.

"With everlasting love have You loved Your people Israel, Teaching us Torah and mitzvot, laws and judgments."
—Ahavat Olam, from the Siddur

In Jewish life, teaching, learning, and loving have always been connected. Learning Torah means growing into the people we are meant to be. To offer the opportunity to learn Torah is to offer someone the possibility of reaching his or her highest potential. If someone truly loves you, he or she sends you to school.

- Why did Rachel want Akiva to go to school even though he was already an adult?

- Is it ever too late to learn?

- We don't often think of providing an education as an expression of love. How would schools be different if we did?

The Storyteller

We all have stories to tell. But none of our stories is complete. That is why we feel compelled to share our stories and listen to other people's stories. In sharing and listening, we begin to find the missing parts of our own life stories.

When the Ba'al Shem Tov, the founder of Hasidism, died, his disciples gathered to distribute his worldly possessions. One was given his tefillin and another, his *shtender*—his lectern. One received his books and another, his cup.

At the end of the line waited one faithful Hasid. But there was nothing of worldly value left, so he was given only the master's stories—and the responsibility of sharing them with the world.

The Hasid was dismayed. He would much rather have received something of tangible value. But he was conscientious and therefore set out into the world to share the master's stories. He didn't starve, but neither did he make much of a living. After all, Jews were poor. And how much could poor Jews pay for even the most enchanting of tales?

So when word came to him that a wealthy Jewish man in a far-off land was prepared to offer a great fortune for the stories of the Ba'al Shem Tov, he praised God for the blessing and set off for the man's estate. Arriving on a Friday afternoon just before Shabbat, he was welcomed with great warmth and escorted directly into a magnificent banquet hall. After dinner the man and his guests turned to the Hasid and begged him to grace the evening with one of the Ba'al Shem Tov's stories.

At that moment the Hasid's mind went blank. Not one story could penetrate the fog, not one anecdote, not one reminiscence—he could remember nothing. In all the years of storytelling, this had never happened. Blushing with embarrassment and stammering in fear, he apologized.

"No matter!" responded the gracious host. "You are no doubt exhausted from your journey. Perhaps tomorrow you will share your stories with us!"

But the same thing happened at Shabbat lunch and again at supper. Just as he was about to begin one of his favorite stories, his mind went blank. Embarrassed, frustrated, and fearing the wealthy man's disappointment, the Hasid decided it best that he sneak away.

As he was slipping out of the palace that night, he was met at the door by his host. "I beg your forgiveness, sir," the startled Hasid pleaded. "I spent years with the Ba'al Shem Tov. I know hundreds of his tales, I have recited them for years, but for some reason I can remember none of them."

"Not one?" begged the man, suddenly distressed. "You were with the Ba'al Shem for so many years. Can't you remember even one moment of your master's life?"

"Only one remains with me," the Hasid replied. "Not a story, but a memory of a time when I was young and first began to follow the master. I was with him on Shabbat. He was distant and gloomy but would tell none of us why. As soon as Shabbat was over, he ordered us into his wagon, and we began a long trip. By morning we had entered a town notorious for its vicious attacks on its Jews. And this was the worst of days to visit, Easter Sunday, when the Christian hatred of Jews was at its very greatest. We entered the town and found the entire Jewish quarter boarded up. No one would open a door to take us in. Finally we found our way to the synagogue's attic.

"In this town there was a bishop famous for his fierce hatred of the Jews. Every Easter the bishop would preach to the town, whipping the Christians into a vicious frenzy that they would let loose on the poor Jews. On that Easter Sunday morning the master ordered me to do the strangest thing: 'Go to the Cathedral,' he told me, 'and tell the bishop that the holy Ba'al Shem is ready to see him.'

"I protested. 'Master,' I said, 'how can I go to such a place! They'll kill me!' I trembled in fear.

"But the master insisted, and so I went. The Christians looked at me in wonder as I ascended the pulpit to deliver the message. When I told the bishop that the holy Ba'al Shem was ready to see him, he turned, left the cathedral, and accompanied me to the synagogue.

"I don't know what happened next. The master and the bishop spent an hour in private conversation. Then the bishop emerged and returned to his pulpit in the cathedral. All I know is that there was no riot and no killing that year. The bishop sent the crowd home and declared the Jewish community under his protection. After that, I heard he disappeared and was never seen again."

At that the Hasid turned his gaze upon his host, who was weeping.

"Thank you, dear brother, thank you," he stammered. "You have no idea what you've done for me tonight. Thank you." He embraced the Hasid as he continued to weep.

At last, he composed himself and explained: "Dear brother, I was that bishop. I was the one who sent the mobs to kill and plunder the Jews of the town. But months before that Easter, I was haunted by strange dreams. I was told that on Easter a holy stranger would come to release me from my nightmares. It was I you summoned that morning to appear before the holy Ba'al Shem.

"In that hour he revealed to me my own secret. I had been born a Jew. I had been stolen from my mother before I could know her and was raised in the Church. I was taught to hate the Jews and to spread that hatred. I rose up in the world, from a poor orphan to the bishop of the region.

"But then the dreams came, and in them were visions of the hell that awaited me. I pleaded with your master: Was there no way for me to repent these terrible sins? And he showed me my only chance: To study Torah and live as a Jew, to open my doors to the poor and the homeless and use all my resources to support the helpless and the abandoned. That I promised to do.

"I begged him: 'Master, how can I know if my repentance has been accepted?' And he told me: 'When one of my disciples comes to you, one who remembers none of his own stories but tells you your story. When you hear your own story, only then will you know that your repentance has been accepted and you are again with God.'

"Tonight, dear brother, you have brought me my story. Tonight I am free."

The Torah contains 613 commandments. The first is P'ru ur'vu umilu et ha'aretz: *"Be fruitful and multiply and fill the earth" (Genesis 1:28). According to the* Sefer Hachinuch, *the last commandment, the 613th, is to write a Torah scroll. Every Jew is commanded to write out his or her own Torah. We are commanded to write the Torah in our own hand. It is not enough to have inherited a Torah from our ancestors. The collective memory must be reshaped, remolded, and reacquired by each of us. It must be our Torah, our truth—not our ancestors'—that we teach our children. But we must be careful: Stories have consequences. What we choose to tell and how we choose to tell it will shape our lives and the lives of those around us.*

- This is a story about stories, about the power of a story to change a life. How many times in the story does the telling of a story change someone's life?

- Is there a story that your family tells that describes who your family is, how they got here, what's important to all of you? When is that story told? Who tells it?

- Have you ever asked your parents or grandparents about their stories, about how they became the people they are, how they met each other, or how they or their parents or their ancestors came to America?

The Bird in the Tree

There are certain things you can make happen in the world. And there are certain things you just have to let happen on their own. You can bake a cake. You can build a house. But you can't force friendship. You can't manufacture love. You can't make a magic moment happen. You can only be ready when such things occur.

Once upon a time there was a king who had a magnificent collection of birds. Behind his royal palace he built a wonderful palace for all his birds. And when he finished a day of ruling the kingdom, he would go into the bird palace, stretch out his arms, and let all the beautiful birds land on him. There were red birds, blue birds, yellow birds, birds that sang, birds that danced. Every beautiful bird in the world lived in his bird palace—except one.

One day a traveler came to the king and told him of the most beautiful bird in the world. This bird had all the colors of the rainbow on its feathers. And its song was the most magnificent in all the world. But no one could catch this bird. For he lived on the top of the tallest tree in the forest. And he was not only the most beautiful, but he was also the most clever bird in the world.

"I'll catch him!" vowed the king. "I know more about catching birds than anyone else. I'll catch him and bring him to live in my bird palace."

So off the king went, deep into the forest, with his bird-catching equipment and the resolve to capture the most beautiful, most clever bird in the world. Soon he arrived at the center of the forest, where the tallest trees grew. He took out his bird binoculars and looked upward. Sure enough, there he saw the most beautiful bird in the world, with all the colors of the rainbow on its feathers.

The king looked up at the bird and vowed, "I'm coming to get you."

The bird looked down at the king and snickered.

The king removed a long rope from his bag. He formed the end into a lasso and began to swing the rope over his head. Around and around went the rope until it was moving very fast, and then, all of a sudden, he threw it to the top of the tree.

When the bird saw the rope with the lasso coming, he did a little hop to the side. The rope went over the top of the tree and came crashing down—right onto the head of the king.

The bird looked down at the king, now rubbing his sore head, and snickered. The king looked up at the bird and vowed, "I'm coming to get you."

The king took out his bird-catching net. "This never fails," he muttered to himself. He swung the net over his head. Around and around went the net until it was moving very fast, and then, all of a sudden, he threw it all the way up to the top of the tree.

When the bird saw the net coming, he did a little hop to the side. The net went over the top of the tree and came crashing down—right onto the head of the king.

The bird looked down at the king, now rubbing his really sore head, and laughed a snickering laugh.

The king looked up at the bird and vowed, "I'm coming to get you."

The king knew what he needed to do. So out of his bag he took his folding ladder. He opened it and opened it and opened it, until it reached from the ground all the way up to the treetop. Up the ladder climbed the king until he was standing nose to nose with the bird.

"I've come to take you home with me!" he declared.

But the bird shook his head and laughed a snickering laugh. When the king reached out to grab the bird, the bird did a little hop to the side. The king lost his balance and fell off the ladder. Down, down, down, he crashed through the branches, all the way down to the ground.

Now the king was really hurt. His body hurt from falling out of the tree. And his heart hurt because he was out of tricks, and he knew there was no way to catch that bird. So the king sat down beside the tree, and he cried.

While he was crying, a circus rolled up the road. A troupe of acrobats stopped. The leader of the troupe approached the crying king. He put his hand on the king's shoulder and tried to comfort him. He spoke with a strange accent, but his feelings were sincere. "Why are you crying, my friend? Maybe we can help you. We are world-famous acrobats: the Flying Fettuccine Brothers."

The king explained his problem: He loved birds. He collected birds from all over the world. The world's most beautiful bird lived at the top of this tall tree, but this bird could not be caught. What else could he do but cry?

"What else? Let us help you! We do magic every night and matinees on Sundays!"

"Help me? How could you help? The bird is at the top of this tree, and no one can get him down!" explained the king.

"That's all you need? To get the bird from the top of the tree to the bottom? That's no problem for the world-famous Flying Fettuccine Brothers! My brothers will make a human ladder up to the top. And I will climb up and get your bird!"

He called out to his brothers. First came the biggest brother. His name was Lasagna. Lasagna planted himself at the bottom of the tree. Then came Manicotti, who climbed up on his brother's shoulders. Then up on his shoulders climbed Linguine. And on *his* shoulders, Rigatoni. Then Ravioli, Tortellini, Cannelloni, and Capellini. And finally the last brother, Penne, climbed up. All the way to the top he went until he was nose to nose with the bird.

"Mr. Bird," Penne said in his strange accent, "I am coming all the way up here to get you for the king down there. So hold still." Even the bird could not believe this sight.

Then, all of a sudden, the brother at the bottom, the one they called Lasagna, remembered something awful: He was allergic to birds. And indeed he started to sniffle and to grimace, and from deep within him began one huge sneeze. "A-a-a—"

All the other brothers pleaded, "No, Lasagna, not now! Hold it in! Hold it back! No, Lasagna!"

But when a sneeze is ready, nothing in the world can hold it back.

"A-a-a-chooooooooooooooooo!"

As he sneezed, he lost his balance, and all the brothers came tumbling down. Down came Manicotti. Down came Linguine. Down came Rigatoni. Down came Ravioli, Tortellini, Cannelloni, and Capellini. And down came poor Penne. They crashed with a thud.

The king watched all this, and he began to laugh. It was the funniest thing he'd ever seen. He laughed and he laughed until all the Fettuccine Brothers had begun to laugh too. The whole lot of them were lost in laughter.

The king laughed so hard that he didn't notice the bird flying out of the tree and then flying around and around in big circles. He didn't notice that it landed right on his shoulder. The king just kept on laughing. And the bird laughed with him. And the Fettuccine Brothers laughed with them both.

"Did you see that?" the king giggled to the bird. "Did you see how the one on the bottom sneezed? And the whole lot of them came crashing down!" He laughed even louder. And the bird laughed right with him.

Suddenly the king realized that the bird was sitting on his shoulder. He stopped laughing and stared at the bird. "You're here!" he said.

"Of course I'm here. I couldn't let you laugh alone! That was just too funny!" the bird replied.

"But I tried to catch you," said the king.

"You can't catch me!" said the bird. "I won't let you catch me. But if you ask me, I will be your friend."

"You will be my friend?" asked the astonished king. "And will you come home with me and stay in my bird palace?"

"Certainly," answered the bird, "If you invite me, it would be my pleasure."

So the king invited the bird to accompany him home. The bird accepted the invitation, and to this very day he lives in the bird palace behind the royal palace of the king. At the end of each day, when the king is worn out and tired of ruling his kingdom and saddened by the woes of the world, he wanders out to the bird palace. Then, from high up in a great tree circles the most beautiful bird in the world, a bird with all the colors of the rainbow on his feathers. The bird lands upon the shoulder of his friend the king and whispers into the ear of the king: "Remember that time when those guys stood one on top of the other, all the way up the tree—and the big one at the bottom let out a huge sneeze—and down they all came, one on top of the other!"

Then the king and the bird laugh with joy. And their laughter fills the world, because there is nothing as sweet as two friends sharing laughter and life.

According to an old Yiddish proverb, "Man plans and God laughs." The question is, What kind of laughter is God's? Does God laugh at us, ridiculing our plans and aspirations? Or does God laugh with us, enjoying the never-ending drama of human life and all its irony?

- Why didn't the bird let the king catch him? What was he waiting for?

- How many different kinds of laughter are there in this story? Which kind is the best?

- What are some of the things you can't force but must instead wait for and be ready for?

The Rabbi and the Gladiator

Sometimes all it takes to change a life is a momentary meeting: We see something special or we are seen in a special way, and everything suddenly looks different. Sometimes it takes another person to help us see who we really are.

S omewhere in the north of Israel sometime in the second century, two men met on a narrow bridge that crossed a rushing stream. One was named Simon. Simon was an orphan, born of a Jewish family but kidnapped by the Romans and raised to be a gladiator, a fighter in the Roman arena. Simon was a mountain of a man. He was stronger, fiercer, and more feared than any other champion in the Roman Empire. No one could withstand his might and his rage.

Simon was in a hurry to get to his next contest. Across the bridge he rushed, wearing the armor and weapons of a gladiator. At the center of the bridge, his way was blocked by another man, a different kind of champion.

Rabbi Yochanan was a small man with fine features and gentle eyes. The leader of the Jewish community in the Land of Israel, he was renowned for his deep learning and love of Torah. The rabbi wore no armor and carried no weapons. He carried only a scroll of ancient wisdom.

The two men met at the center of the bridge. Simon was in a terrible hurry, so he demanded that the rabbi move aside and let him pass. But the rabbi would not budge. Simon shouted a command: "Move aside!" But still the rabbi would not move. So Simon bellowed and stomped. He reached for his sharpest sword and threatened the rabbi: "If you will not move on your own, I will feed you to the fish of the stream!" But the rabbi held his place.

The gladiator raised his sword. But just as he was about to bring it down on the rabbi, the men's eyes met. And something amazing happened. Simon, the greatest gladiator in all the arenas of the Roman Empire, was accustomed to seeing fear in the eyes of his adversaries. He was accustomed to seeing terror in the faces of his rivals, the kind of paralyzing terror that alone enabled him to defeat his foes. But not this day. Not this time. Simon saw something in the eyes of the rabbi he had never seen before. He saw absolutely no fear. He saw in the eyes of the rabbi a man who knew exactly where he fit in God's world, a man who knew exactly what he was sent into the world to do. He saw in the rabbi's eyes a strength and a power he had never seen in all his opponents in all the battles in all the arenas of Rome. The power of the rabbi's eyes shook Simon to his soul. He stood for a long time staring, and then he dropped his sword and let go of all his rage. He was absorbed by the gentle face of the great rabbi.

For his part, the rabbi saw something remarkable in the eyes of the gladiator. There was much more to this gladiator than his fury. Beyond all the bluster and rage and violence, the rabbi saw in the gladiator's eyes a ferocious power to love and a deep longing to be loved. Behind the armor was a heart, a soft human heart. Behind the armor was a soul waiting to be touched, to be warmed.

The rabbi spoke softly to the gladiator. He said, "My brother, where are you going in such a hurry? To kill or be killed in the service of Roman glory? My brother, let me show you a different way, a way to a greater glory."

"There is no glory greater than Rome! Rome is eternal! I serve only Caesar!" The gladiator repeated the oath he had sworn many times.

"One day soon Rome will be gone, its Caesars forgotten and all its arenas reduced to rubble," explained the rabbi. "But the glory of God is forever. And you, my brother, are created in the image of God. You carry God's light. That is the word of God's Torah. You should serve no Caesar and no empire. God's Torah is the only decree anyone should put above himself! Come and join a greater cause, my brother. Come and master God's Torah!"

"I know only the arts of battle. How can I sit with a scholar like you?" the gladiator retorted with embarrassment.

"Your heart is stronger than your sword, and that is all God requires. Come, my brother," answered the rabbi.

Perhaps it was the rabbi's truth. Perhaps it was his gentle, loving voice. Perhaps it was that the rabbi was the first person ever to call him brother. Whatever the reason, the rabbi's words broke through the gladiator's armor and reached his heart. For the first time in his life, the gladiator began to cry. Tears covered his face, and his sobs filled the valley. He dropped his weapons into the stream. He unbuckled and cast away his armor. He turned and followed the rabbi.

Simon became Rabbi Yochanan's most devoted student, and in time the gladiator, too, became a rabbi, the great Reish Lakish. He married the sister of Rabbi Yochanan and became his brother-in-law. They fought and wrestled over the words of Torah for the rest of their lives as they led the Jewish people with love and with learning.

"The righteous bloom like a date palm;
They thrive like a cedar in Lebanon;
Planted in the house of the Lord,
They flourish in the courts of our God."
—Psalm 92:13–14

Many truths claim us. The question is, which truths allow us to become the people we are meant to be? Which will give us lives of purpose and meaning? Which give us the courage to meet life's difficulties with hope? Which will fulfill our deepest desires?

Sometimes our decisions go against the accepted wisdom of our time. In order to follow the rabbi, the gladiator had to give up his fame, status, and power in Rome. But he gained something more valuable: He recovered himself and gained an immortality in the pages of the Talmud.

- What did the gladiator see in the rabbi's eyes that changed his heart and his mind?

- What did the rabbi see in the gladiator that revealed the gladiator's potential?

- What is real strength? Is it a matter of muscles and physical power? Or is there another kind of strength that makes us even more powerful?

Hidden Truths

✴

Rabbi Isaac taught, "The light created by God in the Beginning flared from one end of the world to the other, and then it was hidden away." Rabbi Judah taught, "Every single day a ray of that light shines into the world."

(Zohar 1:31b–32)

Lift Up Your Eyes and See

The Passover Haggadah prompts us all to ask a very good question: What if we were slaves and we didn't even know it? What if what enslaved us was not a Pharaoh in Egypt but a way we've grown accustomed to living? How can we free ourselves?

Among the many Israelites who left Egypt were two men: Sh'lumi'el and Buz.

Slaves never look up; they only look down. And as slaves for their entire lives, Sh'lumi'el and Buz had grown so accustomed to looking down they could no longer lift their eyes.

When Moses brought us across the Red Sea, we all witnessed the great miracle: The sea parted, and we escaped from slavery. We became a free people. We came to know that God has a purpose in our history.

Sh'lumi'el asked Buz, "What do you see?"

"I see mud," Buz responded.

"I see mud, too. What's all this about freedom? We had mud in Egypt; we have mud here!"

And they missed the miracle of their escape. The sea split before them, but they didn't see it. They saw only mud.

Then we stood at Mount Sinai in the Presence of God and heard God's voice proclaiming the commandments. We accepted God's Covenant and pledged ourselves to become a holy people, God's partners in healing the world.

Sh'lumi'el asked Buz, "What do you hear?"

"I hear someone shouting commands," Buz answered.

"I hear commands, too. What's all this about Torah? They shouted commands in Egypt; they shout commands here."

And they missed the miracle of hearing God's voice. God spoke to every Israelite, but Sh'lumi'el and Buz didn't hear His voice. They had heard enough commands.

Finally, after forty years of wandering in the desert, we arrived at the Promised Land, the land of milk and honey, the land promised our ancestors. We arrived in the place of our fondest dreams.

Buz asked Sh'lumi'el, "How do you feel?"

"My feet hurt," Sh'lumi'el replied.

"My feet hurt, too. What's all this about a Promised Land? My feet hurt in Egypt; my feet hurt here!"

And they missed the miracle of entering our own land, Eretz Yisrael. The Israelites returned to the land promised them by the Covenant. The promise to our ancestors was fulfilled, but Sh'lumi'el and Buz didn't know it—they knew none of it. Their feet hurt too much.

So what did they do? Sh'lumi'el and Buz turned around and began walking back toward Egypt.

Some say that Sh'lumi'el and Buz are still wandering in the wilderness, looking down at the desert sand and rocks and complaining to each other.

Others say they went back to Egypt. Back to Pharaoh. Back to slavery. Back to the place they knew best. Back to the place where they began.

Still others say they've seen Sh'lumi'el and Buz—or perhaps their descendants—walking among us, living right here and now, wandering about with their eyes cast down, missing all the miracles that are taking place around them all the time. They haven't any idea where they're going. And they continue to miss all the many chances to know what life is about.

If only they could lift up their eyes and see!

In Hebrew, Egypt is Mitzrayim, *literally, "the narrow place."* Mitzrayim *is not only a physical place; it is also a description of a kind of life—a life so constricted and narrow no truth can seep in. The worst form of slavery isn't defined solely by chains, shackles, whips, or taskmasters. The worst form of slavery is a slavery of the mind, in which the slave accepts his or her slavery and can imagine no other way of living. It is a slavery so deep the slave doesn't even realize that he or she is a slave and refuses to accept any attempts at liberation. Even in a world without a Pharaoh and without taskmasters, such slavery is all too common.*

- What makes a person a slave? What would it take to free someone who is enslaved?

- In what ways do we act like Sh'lumi'el and Buz? What parts of life do we miss by looking down? What might it take to get us to look up?

- How does the Torah teach us to look up and be free?

Finding God

Many people think that religion is about secrets—secrets to life, to happiness, to success. But wisdom isn't a secret. It cannot be purchased or stolen or read in a book. It is acquired by experiencing life and thinking deeply about what life has to teach.

Once there was a boy who asked questions. From the time he was very young, he questioned everyone about everything. His questions never stopped; every answer only gave birth to a new question. He began asking about small things. And as he grew older, his questions grew bigger. So by the time he was a young man, he sought the biggest answers of all. But there was no one in his small village who could answer those questions.

"You must go and see the rebbe," his father told him. "He will help you find your answers."

The rebbe was a great teacher. He knew the answers to the biggest of questions. He even knew the secrets of God. So the boy's mother packed his bag, and with a hug of love his parents sent him on his way.

The boy arrived in the rebbe's town and found his way to the rebbe's school. He listened intensely to the rebbe's lessons, thrilled at the prospect of finally finding answers. At last he was shown in to see the rebbe.

"Great Rebbe, please teach me about God!" the boy pleaded. "I want to learn the secrets of God."

The rebbe stared at the boy's face for some time and at last responded, "I will teach you. But tell me, do you have a place to stay?"

"A place to stay?" the boy asked. "I don't need a place to stay! I want to master the secrets of God!"

"Yes, of course. But first go and find a place to stay. Then you'll learn the secrets."

The boy left the rebbe's presence. He wasn't happy about the delay, but he knew he must obey the rebbe.

He scoured the town, searching for an inn, a room, a loft, even a spare bed. He found nothing available. It was a small town. No one had a room to spare. If he wanted to stay in the town, he would have to build a place for himself. So he found a good-hearted carpenter, who offered to share his skills and lend his tools. And the boy set to work building a home. He didn't know if he could do it since he had never built anything before. But he knew he must try. For only then would the rebbe share his secrets.

It wasn't easy. Each time he put up a wall, it fell down. And each time he covered the roof, it fell in. But he persisted. Finally the walls stayed up. And the roof stayed up. And the windows and doors opened and shut. And the boy realized that he had built himself a home! It wasn't big. It wasn't pretty. But it was cozy and warm, and it was his! He had never thought he could do such a thing, but he'd done it. So he returned to the rebbe.

"Rebbe, I built myself a home. I would never have believed I could do such a thing, but I mastered the skills, and now I have a home. Now, please, teach me the secrets of God!"

The rebbe looked into the boy's face for some time. Finally he said, "Of course. But first, tell me, do you have a job?"

"A job?" the boy asked. "No, I came to learn the secrets. I have no need for a job!"

"Go and find a job, and then we'll have plenty of time to learn together!"

The boy left the rebbe. He knew he must obey the wise teacher if he ever hoped to learn the secrets of God. So he looked for a job.

The village baker was advertising for an apprentice. The boy offered himself. He had never worked so hard in his life. From early in the morning until late in the night, until his hands were weary and his back ached and his head hurt. But he learned. He learned how to turn flour and water into fine loaves of bread and sweet cakes. He learned the joy of serving his neighbors. And when he had mastered the trade, the village baker made him a partner. On that day the boy took a basket of his best breads and cakes and brought them to the rebbe.

"Rebbe, you told me to find a place to stay, so I built a home. You told me to get a job, so I learned to bake. Look, I have brought you the fruits of my labors! Now, please, share with me the secrets I have waited so long to hear!"

The rebbe looked long into the boy's face. Finally he asked, "Are you married?"

"Married?" asked the boy with obvious frustration. "Why should I be married? I came to learn the great secrets of God, not to get married!"

"Of course," said the rebbe. "But first, go and get married. Then you'll learn the secrets."

The boy was frustrated. He was angry. But what was he to do? How could he argue with the rebbe?

In the town there was a girl he liked, and he suspected she liked him. So he began to spend time with her. They took walks at sunset. And had picnics in the meadow. They talked about their dreams. And they fell in love. In his whole life he had never known he could love someone as much as he loved her. He asked her to marry him, and she asked him to marry her. Their wedding was simple but warmed by their love. She moved into his cozy home, and they shared the fruits of their labors.

The boy returned to the rebbe. "Rebbe, you told me to find a place to live, so I built a home. You told me to find a job, so I learned a trade. Then you asked me to get married. I found a woman. I never knew I could love anyone as much as I love her. We are married. Now, Rebbe, please, teach me the secrets of God."

"Do you have children?" the rebbe asked.

Somehow, the boy expected this. He wasn't nearly as frustrated as before. This time he just smiled. "No, not yet, but if you tell me, I will obey."

"Good," said the rebbe. "Go and have children. Then come back, and I will teach you!"

In his whole life, he had never thought he could love someone as much as he loved his wife. He had never thought he could work so hard as he worked at his trade. And he had never thought he would feel as good as the day his home was complete. But then the children came. And the boy discovered that he could love even deeper and work even harder and feel even more complete than he ever had felt before. He cared for his family and gave them everything he had and everything he made. And yet he felt more happiness than he had ever known.

So he returned to the rebbe.

"Great Rebbe, when I came to you years ago, I asked you to teach me the secrets of God. You told me to find a place to stay; you told me to find a job; you told me to get married; then you told me to have children. Now, Rebbe, I am ready. I have done everything you asked. Now, please, teach me the secrets of God."

The rebbe stared into the boy's face. "Not yet. You're not ready yet."

"But what else do you require?" the boy cried. "What else?"

"Soon you will know." And with that, the rebbe turned back to his books.

Soon after, a messenger came from the boy's village with an urgent message. The boy's grandfather was ill. The boy was needed at once.

The boy rushed home. He found his grandfather weary and sick. He sat with his grandfather, and they talked, sharing all that life had taught them. And when the grandfather realized that his grandson had grown into a man, learned and wise, he smiled weakly, fell asleep, and peacefully died with his grandson beside him.

The boy cried with a sadness he had never felt before. He loved his grandfather and missed him so much. He knew no way to escape his loneliness and pain. He asked himself how he could ever feel good again, how he could ever find a way back to life.

But as the days went by, sweet memories of his grandfather replaced some of his pain. And he found the way back to life, to his family, to his happiness, to the rebbe.

"Great Rebbe," he declared, "I loved my grandfather so much. I never thought I could say good-bye. I never thought I could ever overcome my sadness and pain. But my grandfather taught me to love life as he did. And so I have found a way to remember him and yet feel happy. Am I ready now to share the secrets of God?"

"Yes, my son. Now you are ready to hear the secrets." The rebbe took a deep breath. He stood and walked to the window. He stared at the sunset outside.

"You came here years ago looking for a God outside yourself—far away, up in the universe. But the best place to find God is within: in your ability to grow, to learn, to build, to produce, to love, to share, to care, and to overcome life's pain. You need no more secrets. You have already found the God you came looking for. My son, you already know the secrets."

The boy listened to every word. He knew the rebbe was right. Had he heard these words years before, when he first arrived, he would have slammed his fist down in frustration. But now, having done all the rebbe had asked—having built a home, and made a living, and loved a wife, and cared for a family, and said goodbye to his grandfather—he knew in his heart that the rebbe was right. All the secrets he needed were his already.

The boy remained the rebbe's student and disciple for many years. And when the rebbe was old and in need of rest, he turned to the boy and appointed him rebbe in his place.

The new rebbe humbly assumed his position. Soon his reputation had spread far and wide throughout the land: The new rebbe was wise beyond compare. He knew all the answers to all the questions. He could answer even the biggest of questions—he knew the secrets of God.

People came from all over seeking the rebbe's wisdom. And when any young person would come and say to the rebbe, "Teach me, please, the secrets of God," the rebbe would look into his face for a long while and then reply, "Do you have a place to stay? Go, find a place. Then I'll share the secrets with you!"

✦

> *"[Moses] said, 'Oh, let me see Your essence!'*
> *[God] answered, 'I will make all My goodness pass before you,*
> *and I will proclaim before you the name Lord....But,' God said,*
> *'you cannot see My face, for none may see Me and live.' The Lord*
> *said, 'See, there is a place near Me. Station yourself on the rock, and*
> *as My Presence passes by, I will put you in a cleft of the rock and shield*
> *you with My hand until I have passed by. Then I will take My hand*
> *away, and you will see My back; but My face must not be seen.'"*
> —Exodus 33:18–23

The boy's question is the question asked by every religious person: "What is God?" Even Moses wants to see God's glory. And God's answer to Moses is much like the rebbe's response to the boy: You can't know God by looking directly into the mystery. You know God by finding the place where God has been. The rebbe sent the boy to seek the Presence of God in his own experiences of transcendence. In becoming more than we are, in building, planting, loving, creating, and renewing, we can feel the Presence of God in our lives.

- Why didn't the rabbi just tell the boy the secrets of God?

- What kinds of experiences did the rabbi want the boy to have? Were they happy or sad? Simple or profound? What did the young man learn from each experience?

- In what ways do we learn about God?

The Magic Ring

We live in time. Time has the magic power to heal our hurts, brighten our joys, and deepen our most splendid moments—but only if we understand its magical power and learn to appreciate it.

There was once a king who had the most magnificent collection of jewels in the entire world. It was the source of his greatest joy. He prided himself on having collected the best and the finest of the world's gems. Hour after hour he would admire and enjoy his jewels.

One night the king had a dream. He dreamed that somewhere in the world there was a ring, the most precious ring in the world. This ring had special power: When a person was sad, it could make her happy; when a person was giddy and drunk, it could sober him and bring him back to himself; and when a person was joyful, it intensified and heightened her joy.

The king awoke from his dream convinced that somewhere in the world such a ring existed. He felt compelled to have it, so he called together his advisers and ministers and servants and described the dream to them. He offered a fabulous reward to the one who found the ring. He was prepared to pay any price.

Each of the advisers and ministers and servants went out in search of the ring, and each returned empty-handed. Except one, whose love for his master pushed him onward. Years went by. He scoured the world, searching every gallery, every shop, and every bazaar, to no avail. After years of searching, he, too, returned empty-handed.

But before he would confess his failure to his master, the king, the servant stopped one last time at a shop close to the palace. He described to the owner what he was seeking and described, too, all his trials of the past years.

The owner, an old man, simply smiled. "I have the ring," he told the minister. "Come, let me get it for you."

"You have it?" exclaimed the astonished servant, remembering all the years of his arduous search. "You possess the magic ring?"

"Yes," answered the old man. "It was given to me by a wise man many years ago. Somehow I knew that one day someone would come for it, but until now no one has asked for it. No one has ever appreciated its remarkable magic. Here, I'll get it for you."

He took down an old box, opened the lid, and removed a soft brown cloth. He unfolded the cloth, and the servant saw a simple metal ring. It was not gold or silver, and it was not adorned with gems. The old man handed the ring to the astonished servant.

"I will pay you whatever you ask," said the servant. "Whatever fortune you ask is yours!"

"No," replied the old man. "Your king needs this ring. Take it as my gift."

The servant rushed to the palace. He entered the king's chamber, approached the throne, bowed low to his master, and announced, "Your Majesty, I have found your magic ring. Years of searching have yielded fruit: The miraculous ring is yours."

He presented the ring to the king. The king opened the box and unfolded the cloth. He examined the plain, unadorned metal ring. Could this be the precious magic ring? Then he saw that three Hebrew words were engraved on it: *Gam zeh ya'avor.* "This too shall pass."

Over time the king came to realize the magical power of the ring. When he was sad, he would look upon it and it would remind him that *this too shall pass.* And he would be consoled as he recalled that dawn always follows the darkness of night. When he was giddy and drunk, he would look upon the ring and be reminded that *this too shall pass.* And he would be sobered, brought back to his senses. And when he experienced true joy, real happiness, the ring reminded him that *this too shall pass.* The king learned to hold on to and appreciate those precious moments. Soon he realized that this ring was indeed the most valuable ring in the world. He lost interest in the rest of his collection: All his many jewels and gems paled in comparison with the plain metal ring, which never left his hand.

At the Passover seder, just before we eat the meal, we taste koreich, *the "Hillel sandwich." Hillel, the first-century sage, combined the symbolic foods of the seder to fulfill the Torah's commandment. In this act, in the eating of* koreich, *we taste something special. In eating the* matzah, *the biting, bitter* maror, *and the sweet* charoset *all together, we taste life— and the taste of life is bittersweet. The* charoset *mellows the sting of the* maror, *making it digestible. The* maror *brings out the sweetness of the* charoset. *Bittersweet is the flavor of a life lived in full awareness of the passage of time. The passage of time offers comfort when we suffer. The passage of time sobers us when we are giddy. Most of all, the awareness of time teaches us to cherish the gift of sweet, miraculous moments, when they occur in our lives.*

- When the king was sad, what did the ring tell him?

- When the king was joyful, what did the ring tell him?

- When he was foolish, what did it tell him?

The Diamond

Before the world was created, God created t'shuva, the power to change, for without t'shuva none of us could exist. T'shuva isn't easy. It isn't easy acknowledging that something we did was wrong. It isn't easy apologizing for a mistake. And it certainly isn't easy changing ourselves. The rabbis taught that one who does t'shuva—turning from wrong to right—has attained greater moral stature than one who has never known sin, error, or failure. The only whole heart, they taught, is a broken one.

There once was a king who had a magnificent collection of jewels. Among his jewels was his very favorite: a great, perfect diamond. After each long, hard day of governing the kingdom, settling conflicts, and making difficult decisions, he would retreat to his private chambers to meditate on the perfection of this diamond. The diamond brought the king great joy. Caressing its surfaces, gazing upon its facets, he concluded that the diamond was proof that something perfect could exist in this world. Everything else in life was compromised.

One night a tragedy occurred. While the king was caressing the diamond, it fell from his hands and careened through the air, smashing onto the stone floor. With trembling fingers, he picked it up and peered into its interior. To his horror, the king perceived a long spindle of a crack running from the very top to the very bottom of the gem. The king was distraught. The diamond was flawed, its perfection forever ruined. He grieved over the broken jewel, the last perfect thing in all Creation. He was inconsolable. The ministers and servants of the king, seeking to comfort him, brought all sorts of experts to the royal court to repair the diamond. Jewelers, gemologists, scientists, technicians, and even wizards were engaged. All failed to repair the crack.

Finally, there came one wise old craftsman. He looked carefully into the diamond for a long time, then looked up into the face of the king. "Give me a week, and I will repair your diamond," he announced.

"You can repair it? So many others have tried and failed," the king responded sadly.

"Give it to me for a week, and I will bring it back more perfect than before."

"More perfect?" echoed the astonished king.

"Yes, more perfect."

The king, intrigued by the offer, handed the precious gem to the craftsman. Within the week the craftsman had returned.

"Have you fixed it?" asked the king anxiously.

"I have," replied the craftsman. "It is once again perfect. In fact, it is more perfect than before."

He handed the diamond to the king. The king lifted it to the light. And there was the crack, just as it had been before—long, spindly, marring the perfection of the gem from its very top to its very bottom.

"Do you mock me? It is still broken! It is still flawed!" roared the desperate king.

"Look again," said the craftsman, and he turned the diamond over.

The king again held it up to the light. And now he saw: At the top, where the crack met the tip of the diamond, the craftsman had carved a tiny rose. Now, instead of a long, ugly crack marring the perfection of the gem, the diamond had within it the most exquisite flower, with a long, magnificent stem running through the stone from its top to its bottom.

"Here, my lord," offered the craftsman, "it is not only repaired, but in truth it is now unique, more remarkable, more perfect than before."

When Moses brought the Tablets of the Law down from Mount Sinai, he saw the Israelites worshipping the Golden Calf. He dropped the tablets, and they shattered. After the people repented, God invited Moses to carve new tablets. But what happened to the broken pieces of the first set of tablets? The rabbis taught, "The broken tablets were placed into the Holy Ark, alongside the new, whole tablets" (Talmud Bava Batra 14b).

We carry our brokenness together with our wholeness. The brokenness together with the wholeness is what makes us complete. For it takes great courage to admit that we are wrong, to acknowledge our capacity to sin, err, and destroy, and to find the resolution to try again. To do all that is to achieve true greatness.

- In what way has the diamond become more perfect than before?

- How did the craftsman repair the cracked diamond?

- Have you ever had to repair a friendship or "fix" something you said or did? How did you do it? How did it feel when you were done? What did you learn from the experience?

Hiding God's Image

There is no part of you that is more characteristic and more closely tied to your identity than your face. And yet without the aid of a mirror, you cannot see your own face. The essence of your personality, your qualities, your very self—all is hidden from you. It takes great wisdom to know yourself honestly.

In the beginning, God created all the animals—the fish, the birds, and the bugs. But when it came to the human being, God decided to proceed in a different manner. Unlike every other creature in the world, the human being would be given a special gift: The human being would be created in God's image.

God revealed this plan to the angels.

The angels were outraged. How can something as pure, as precious, and as powerful as God's own image be entrusted to a creature as evil and as deceitful and as corrupt as the human being?

If human beings possess God's image, the angels reasoned, they will think the way God thinks, feel what God feels, create as God creates. They will imagine that they are God and rule the world with tyranny and egotism. Human beings will demand that all creatures worship them. They will think it their right to impose their will on other human beings, and they will terrorize all of Creation. Human beings will most certainly destroy all that God has made and ruin all that God loves. We cannot let that happen!

So they decided to save God from this folly: They stole God's image.

Once they possessed the holy image, they knew it had to be concealed somewhere, hidden in a place where humanity would never find it. But where?

"Let us put it at the top of the highest mountain!" one angel suggested.

"But no. One day they will learn to climb the mountain and find it."

"Then let us put it at the bottom of the sea!" another offered.

"But no. They will find a way to plumb those depths one day, and they will find it."

"Let it be hidden at the farthest reach of the most forbidding wilderness!" suggested another angel.

"But no. One day they will traverse the wilderness and find it."

They all offered suggestions, but each one was rejected. And then the cleverest, shrewdest of the angels stepped forward and said, "No, not at the top of the mountains, nor at the bottom of the sea, nor at the farthest reaches of the wilderness. Let us place it where human beings will never look for it. Let us place it deep within their hearts, deep in their souls. They'll never go looking for it there!"

So God allowed the angels to hide the precious image deep within the heart of the human being. And to this day it lies hidden in a place that is deeper and farther away than any place any one of us can find on our own—but not so deep and not so far away that someone who knows us and loves us can't reach it easily and cherish it.

The philosopher Abraham Joshua Heschel pointed out a contradiction in the Bible: The Ten Commandments prohibit us from making an image of God out of any material in the world. But God seems to have violated this very commandment by creating the human being in God's own image. How can that be? It's not that God has no image. This contradiction teaches that there is only one material in the world that can be fashioned into an image of God, and that is a whole human life. But doing so demands that we discover what is truly divine in our character.

- Why were the angels afraid to give the image of God to human beings? Were they right? Why or why not?

- How did God protect God's image from the destructive capacities of human beings?

- How is it possible that another person, a person who loves us, can know us better than we might ever know ourselves?

PART SIX

The Miracle of Jewish Life

I will make of you a great nation,
And I will bless you;
I will make your name great,
And you shall be a blessing.

(Genesis 12:2)

The Magician

Something magical happens in Jewish homes on Passover. We gather to celebrate our blessings and tell a great story of hope. We remember how much we mean to one another. We remember to notice the blessings of our lives. We are transformed as if by magic.

There once was a very old man and a very old woman who lived in a very old house at the edge of a very old village. They were so very poor, but they were happy, content with all that God had given them.

As Pesach drew closer, the very old woman said to the very old man, "Go into the village and buy wine and matzah and all that we need so that we may have a seder."

But the very old man replied, "We have no money for wine or for matzah, nor for any of the things we need for a seder."

"Very well," the very old woman said. "We have each other, our love and our memories, and that will be enough for the holiday."

So on the seder night, when families the world over gathered at beautiful tables set with wine and matzah and all the special foods of Pesach, the very old man and the very old woman sat in their tiny home at a bare, empty table in the dark. They held hands and sang the songs of the seder slowly and with a little sadness:

> *Dai-dai-yeinu,*
> *Dai-dai-yeinu,*
> *Dai-dai-yeinu,*
> *Dai-yeinu, dai-yeinu.*

Suddenly there was a knock at the door.

"Who could that be?" asked the very old woman.

The very old man opened the door. There stood a stranger, a tall man with a very tall hat and a long coat. He had shining blue eyes and a long beard that came to a point in the middle of his chest.

The stranger spoke with a strange accent. "Good evening," said he. "I am a traveler from far away. And I am in need of a place to celebrate the seder tonight."

"We would be honored to have you at our table," the very old man said, opening the door wide, "but please understand, we have so little with which to make the holiday holy."

"No matter," responded the stranger, waving his hand. "I would be privileged to join you!" He entered the tiny house and sat down at the bare, empty table. "Please, continue your seder."

So the very old man took the hand of the very old woman. They smiled at their guest and sang the songs of the seder with a little more joy:

Dai-dai-yeinu,
Dai-dai-yeinu,
Dai-dai-yeinu,
Dai-yeinu, dai-yeinu.

"Wait!" interrupted the stranger. "The tablecloth! Where is the tablecloth for the holiday feast?"

"We have no tablecloth," responded the very old woman sadly.

"But I have a tablecloth! Now where did I leave it?" said the stranger as he felt through his pockets. And suddenly out of a pocket in his coat he produced the most magnificent white lace tablecloth. He whipped it through the air, and it floated perfectly onto the table.

"How did you do that?" asked the very old man in astonishment.

"How did he do that?" asked the very old woman in amazement.

"No matter!" responded the stranger. "Now, where are the candles to sanctify this holiday night? Where are the candles and the candlesticks?"

"We have no candles, nor have we candlesticks," answered the very old woman sadly.

"But I have candles! Now where did I leave them?" asked the stranger, once again searching through the pockets of his great coat. "Ah, yes!" he announced as he pulled out of a pocket two golden candlesticks holding two long white candles that were already lit. "Here they are!"

As he placed the candlesticks on the white tablecloth, the house glowed with a beautiful golden light.

"How did you do that?" asked the very old man in astonishment.

"How did he do that?" asked the very old woman in amazement.

"No matter!" responded the stranger. "Let us continue our seder."

So the very old man took the hand of the very old woman, and they sang the songs of the seder a little louder and a little stronger.

"Wait!" interrupted the stranger. "Where is the wine? How can there be a seder without wine?"

"We had no money for wine this year," the very old man answered with sorrow.

"But I have wine! If I could only remember where…" The stranger searched through his many pockets and produced three golden cups, already filled with sweet wine. "That's better!"

"How did you do that?" asked the very old man in astonishment.

"How did he do that?" asked the very old woman in amazement.

"No matter!" responded the stranger. "But matzah, where could the matzah be?" He reached behind him and out of nowhere produced an elegant china plate stacked with matzah. "Yes, here it is!" he pronounced. "Now let us continue our seder, shall we?"

The very astonished old man took the hand of the very amazed old woman, and they sang the songs of the seder even louder and stronger:

Dai-dai-yeinu,
Dai-dai-yeinu,
Dai-dai-yeinu,
Dai-yeinu, dai-yeinu.

"A seder plate, that's what we need! Where is the seder plate?"

"We have no plate, nor the special foods for the seder," explained the very old woman, her eyes filling with tears.

"But, my friends, I have a seder plate." Again he searched the inside of his great coat, and this time he pulled out a magnificent golden seder plate with all the special foods of the holiday already placed upon it. "Here it is!" he announced with triumph. "*Maror* and *charoset! Z'roa* and *beitzah! Karpas* and *chazeret!* It's all here. So now, my friends, let us sing of freedom and blessings!"

"How did you do that?" asked the very old man in astonishment.

"How did he do that?" asked the very old woman in amazement.

The stranger just waved away the questions and began the song with true spirit:

Dai-dai-yeinu,
Dai-dai-yeinu,
Dai-dai-yeinu,
Dai-yeinu, dai-yeinu.

When the prayers and songs were finished, the stranger rose and asked, "Dinner? What shall we have for the holiday feast?"

"We have no feast. We have no food," the very old man and the very old woman responded.

The stranger only laughed. "Of course not, but I do!"

With that he removed his tall hat and placed it on the table. He reached into the hat and brought out bowls of hot soup with matzah balls, plates of gefilte fish with horseradish, platters of roasted chicken with potatoes and carrot *tzimmes*, bowls of fruit, cups of hot tea, Passover cookies and sweets.

The very old man and the very old woman watched in wonder. "How did you do that?" asked the very old man in astonishment. "How did he do that?" asked the very old woman in amazement. "My friends, let's eat!" the stranger commanded.

And eat they did! A feast greater than any the very old man and the very old woman had eaten in all their lives.

At the end of the feast, it was time to complete the seder. It was time to open the door for Elijah the Prophet, who visits every seder on Pesach night. But the very old man had eaten so much he couldn't stand up to open the door.

The stranger smiled broadly and said, "No matter! I'll get the door." He put his tall hat on his head and went to the door. And together they sang with sweetness:

Eiliyahu haNavi,
Eiliyahu haTishbi,
Eiliyahu, Eiliyahu,
Eiliyahu haGiladi . . .

When the very old man and the very old woman looked up, the stranger was gone. He had disappeared into the night.

"Where did he go?" asked the very old man in astonishment. "Who was he?" asked the very old woman in amazement. "Could it be?" they wondered. "Could he have been Elijah?"

"No matter," they laughed, remembering his words. "Let us sing the songs of the seder and celebrate God's miracles!" And they sang with all their hearts:

Dai-dai-yeinu,
Dai-dai-yeinu,
Dai-dai-yeinu,
Dai-yeinu, dai-yeinu.

> *"In every generation we must see ourselves as if*
> *we personally came out of Egypt."*
> —Mishna Pesachim 10:5

Each year as if by magic the seder brings us back to Egypt to experience the suffering of slavery and to witness again the wonder of liberation. It's not enough to remember or to commemorate. We must go back ourselves and be there. We must taste history. Collective memory must become personal memory because these moments lie at the very heart of all that is Jewish. We know the suffering of the slave, and so we are bound by an ethic that protects each human being. We have seen the sea split, and so we are forbidden to despair of human history and its possibilities.

- What's the real magic of the seder table? What miracles happen year after year at almost every seder?

- Of all the seders in the world, why do you think Elijah came to the seder of the old man and the old woman?

- What was your best seder? Did anything wonderful or magical happen on that night? What was it?

Lifting the Torah

There are many ways in which we show our respect for the Torah. We keep it safe in the synagogue's Ark. We cover it in fine cloth and decorate it with beautiful ornaments. We stand when it is carried. We kiss it when it passes. But there is one way that is more important than all the others: We show the most respect for the Torah when we learn from it.

There once was a city with two synagogues. One synagogue stood in the wealthiest neighborhood. It was an imposing edifice with great golden doors. Inside was a beautiful sanctuary with a great Ark. The Ark itself had two golden doors. And within the Ark were dozens of Torah scrolls, wrapped in golden velvet and adorned with golden crowns.

This synagogue was exceptionally beautiful. It had everything—except congregants. Almost nobody ever visited. No one came to pray or study or celebrate. Except on holidays and very special occasions, the synagogue was empty. Each week the rabbi would come by, open the building, look around to make sure everything was in order, and then close the magnificent building for another week.

The other synagogue was different: It was in the poorest part of town. It was a broken-down hovel of a building with cracked walls and doors that squeaked. But it had congregants, hundreds of them. They came each Shabbat: old people, young people, mothers, fathers, and children. They came because they loved Torah.

The members of this congregation were so poor they couldn't afford a Torah scroll. But they didn't want to admit this to their children. So they took two sticks of wood and a long piece of blank parchment and pretended it was a Torah. They used an old crate covered with an old curtain for an Ark. An old man who was blind served as reader. Years before, he had learned Torah—memorized it, in fact. He could recite the entire Torah by heart. So each week the old man pretended to read from the blank parchment to crowds of people who listened intently, hanging on every word. Between the readings, congregants discussed and argued the meaning of every phrase. Torah was their life, and nothing gave them greater joy than to discover its meanings.

One week the rabbi of the wealthy synagogue arrived at his shul. He opened the great golden doors, switched on the lights, and slowly walked around the stately sanctuary. Everything was in order. Nothing had been disturbed since the week before or the week before that.

As he was about to leave, he heard a noise, a scratching sound. He listened, and then he began to seek out the source of the sound. Was it a bug? a mouse? He searched everywhere until he isolated the source of the sound. It was coming from the Ark. Pressing his ear up against one golden door of the Ark, he listened. Not only did he hear the scratching sound, but he also heard voices within. Voices? Was someone in the Ark? He grasped the huge handles and slowly opened the door, just a crack.

The door swung open, flinging the rabbi back. Out of the Ark came swarms and swarms of letters! Like big black bees, the letters flew off the Torah scrolls and poured out of the Ark. At first the rabbi swatted at them, protecting himself from the onslaught. Then he stopped and watched in amazement.

There was a sharp whistle as a huge black *alef* stepped forward. As the *alef* sounded the order, the letters formed lines in the manner of soldiers: *Alefs* and *bets* and *gimmels* and *dalets* and *hays* began to march in formation to a cadence called out by the huge *alef: "Harep-ta-tum, harep-ta-tum, harep-ta-tum."*

The rabbi couldn't believe his eyes. "Stop!" he yelled. "What are you doing?"

The *alef* signaled the letters to halt, and the lines of letters stood at parade rest. Stepping forward, the *alef* addressed the rabbi. "We're leaving," he declared.

"Leaving?" the rabbi asked, not quite believing he was carrying on a conversation with an *alef*. "Why? Why would you want to leave? Look how we've treated you: We've dressed you in velvet and crowned you in gold. We honor and protect you in this magnificent Ark. We show you our highest reverence and respect."

"It's true, you respect us, Rabbi, but you don't love us. Your Ark is a prison! It's not enough just to dress up a Torah. You must open the Torah and open yourself to Torah! Rabbi, we're lonely! We need people to read us and learn from us and celebrate our teachings."

The rabbi was shocked to hear these words. He pleaded with the letters: "Please, don't leave us! Don't abandon us!"

"Rabbi," replied the *alef* sympathetically, "we're not leaving you. Long ago you left us. We're going where we are appreciated. Now please, Rabbi, move out of the way so we can go."

"I won't!" the rabbi protested in desperation. "I won't move!"

"We don't want to hurt you, Rabbi, but if you don't get out of our way, we'll have to move you."

"Move me? Go ahead and try! I won't let you go!" The rabbi threw his body across the aisle, blocking the doors to the sanctuary.

"Have it your way," responded the *alef*. He whistled for the line of *gimmels* to advance. "One last time, Rabbi, please move."

But the rabbi held his ground.

And then fifty *gimmels*, their kicking feet swinging wildly, charged the rabbi. He held up his hands and ran from the attack. The *alef* whistled the command "forward, march," and the lines of letters advanced.

All the rabbi could do was watch in dazed wonder as the letters jumped off the Torah scrolls, formed lines, and marched in cadence out of his synagogue. At last the final *tav* marched out.

"Where are you going?" the rabbi called out.

The *tav* held out a hand and said, "Follow us!"

So the rabbi followed the army of letters as it marched through the streets and up the avenues and across the town. At last they reached their destination: the doors of the poor synagogue.

It was the moment of the service when the Torah is lifted. The old man stood and slowly hoisted the pretend Torah. As he turned to show the scroll to the congregation, the doors of the synagogue burst open. The congregants gaped in awe as the troops of letters marched in cadence, led by the huge *alef*: "*Harep-ta-tum, harep-ta-tum.*" The old man stood holding the blank Torah aloft, not knowing what had happened. As the letters arrived on the parchment, they found their places, arranging themselves in words and then in verses and finally in columns. The old man felt the Torah become heavier. He set it down and ran his fingers across the parchment. Feeling the letters and the words, he looked up in wonder.

"It's a miracle!" he announced. "Our Torah has become real!"

The congregants surged to the front of the sanctuary to see the real Torah. Someone began a song, and the old man picked up the Torah scroll and began to dance. Soon everyone was dancing and singing and lifting the newly inscribed Torah overhead.

The rabbi stood in the doorway watching the scene. He couldn't believe what he had witnessed: First the letters marching, then the attack of the *gimmels*, and now—dancing with the Torah! He had never seen people dance with a Torah. To him a Torah was heavy, solemn, ponderous. One couldn't dance with a Torah!

The rabbi slowly walked through the room. The weight of his seriousness immediately snuffed out the gaiety. Everyone stopped dancing and singing and stared at the somber-faced rabbi.

"How can you dance with the Torah?" he asked the old reader sternly. "The Torah is holy. The Torah is heavy. The Torah must be revered!"

"How can you *not* dance with it?" answered the reader joyfully. "The Torah is our life, our joy, our gift to our children! Here, hold it in your arms!" And he handed the Torah to the rabbi.

It had been a long, long time since the rabbi had held a Torah. He was surprised: It wasn't heavy at all. He felt the warmth of the Torah infusing his body. A smile came to his lips, and tears came to his eyes. And then he heard a voice from within the scroll, the commanding voice of the *alef:* "Dance!"

His feet moved as someone began a song. He danced around and around, arm in arm with the reader. Soon everyone was dancing and singing, led by the rabbi and the reader. They danced and danced the whole day.

The next Shabbat, as the congregants arrived at the little, poor synagogue for the service, there was the rabbi, sitting in the very first row. As the Torah was read, he strained to catch the depth of each word and to understand every phrase. And when it was time to lift the Torah, the reader called him to the *bimah.* The rabbi again lifted the Torah, and he held it for many minutes. And once it was wrapped, he began the dance again. Around and around he danced, until everyone was dancing with him.

And so to this very day the rabbi from the rich synagogue spends every Shabbat at the poor synagogue, sitting in the very first row, listening intently and pondering each word. He argues with the reader about the deeper meaning of the text and receives the honor of lifting the Torah. He waits to hear the great *alef* issue the order: "Dance!" And dance he does, with the Torah in his arms.

"When Moses took the stone tablets of the Ten Commandments and began down the mountain, the letters and words carried Moses down. But when Moses arrived at the bottom of the mountain and saw the people of Israel dancing around the Golden Calf, the letters and words flew off the tablets. The stone tablets became too heavy for Moses, and he dropped them, and they shattered."
—Midrash Pirkei d'Rabbi Eliezer

Moses was already an old man when he went up Mount Sinai to receive the Torah. How did he manage to climb down the mountain carrying two stone tablets? And when he arrived at the bottom, why did he drop them?

It's not the lovely coverings, the silver and gold ornaments, or even the parchment scroll itself that makes a Torah holy. Torah is holy because the words carry us to heaven. Should we ever lose the words, the whole religion would become too heavy to sustain. Keeping a Torah locked up, even in a golden Ark, away from life and away from those seeking wisdom, is to keep it in prison. And someday every Torah will attempt to break out of such a prison.

- Why did the rabbi think his rich synagogue was taking such good care of his Torahs?

- What did the Torahs think of that rich synagogue?

- What makes a Torah holy?

- Does it show respect to kiss the Torah, stand up when it is carried around, and hold it with reverence yet not learn its words and live its lessons? Why or why not?

The Last Story of the Wise Men of Chelm

Among the wisest and most important characters of the legendary town of Chelm was its beloved rabbi. This story is about him. It is the last story of Chelm. In some ways it is Chelm's saddest story, and in some ways it is its greatest.

hen Moses brought the Israelites across the Red Sea to freedom, they wanted to sing a song to God. But so long had they been slaves to Pharaoh that they had forgotten how to sing. They opened their mouths, but no sound came out. At that moment, God felt their frustration. According to an old midrash, God sent birds from all the corners of the world to teach the Israelites how to sing.

And so it was a custom among the Jews of eastern Europe that each year on *Shabbat Shirah,* the Sabbath when the story of the crossing of the Red Sea is read in the Torah, the children of the synagogue would go outside and spread about crumbs for the birds in gratitude for the gift of song that the birds of the world had shared with the people Israel.

One day in 1948 an old man carrying many huge packages arrived at the port of Haifa. He stood in a long line of people who had come from Europe. They all looked tired and worn from their long journey and from the terrible events that had brought them to the new State of Israel. But they all looked forward to becoming citizens of the new Jewish state.

When the old man approached the immigration officer, he set down his heavy bags and presented his passport.

"Name?" demanded the officer, curtly holding his clipboard and pen ready.

"Elimelech son of Shlomo."

"Occupation?" The officer continued the interrogation without looking up.

"I am a rabbi."

"Name of the city where you last lived?"

"Chelm."

"What was that you said?" The officer looked up from his clipboard. "Where did you say you come from?"

"Chelm. I come from the town of Chelm."

"You come from the town of Chelm, as in the famous Wise Men of Chelm? The ones from the stories we learned as children?" The officer appreciated this bit of humor after his long, dull day.

But the rabbi did not get the joke. He answered quite seriously. "Yes, that's right. I come from Chelm. I am the rabbi of Chelm. Or, rather, I *was* the rabbi of Chelm, before..." A look of sadness crossed the rabbi's face as he remembered what had brought him to Haifa.

The officer did not react to the rabbi's sadness. Instead, he laughed out loud and called out to the other officers in the station. "Hey, everybody, listen to this: We have a celebrity here! He says he's the rabbi of Chelm. You know all the stories of the Wise Men of Chelm? Here is their famous rabbi. The rabbi of Chelm!"

Loud laughter filled the station as all the other officers and many of the passengers crowded around. People gawked and mocked. "The Wise Men of Chelm? Their rabbi is here? Can you believe this?"

Finally the officer returned to his business. "OK, old fellow. Enough jokes," he said. "What is your name, and where have you come from?"

The rabbi explained in all sincerity: "My name is Rabbi Elimelech son of Shlomo, and I really am the rabbi of Chelm. You may laugh at the stories, but they are true. Chelm is—or rather was—a real place. The Wise Men of Chelm were very real. And I was their rabbi!"

The officer looked into the man's eyes and realized that he wasn't going to change his mind. So he wrote down what he was told. "OK, fine," he said. "Have it your way. Elimelech son of Shlomo, rabbi of Chelm. So, Rabbi, what's in all these packages?"

The rabbi looked right back into the face of the officer. "They are cages, filled with birds," he stated.

"Birds?" The officer was even more surprised. "You brought birds all the way from Europe?

"Yes," replied the rabbi, opening one of his bags. "I brought birds."

"Why birds? Were you afraid there were no birds here in Israel? I can assure you we have plenty of birds—"

"No, you don't understand. When the Nazis came, they took everyone. Everyone. The men, the women, the children—everyone was taken away. By some miracle I survived. I was liberated from the concentration camp. And after I was liberated, I went back to my village. I went back to Chelm to see if anyone else had survived. But there was no one. Not one other person from Chelm had survived. I found myself alone. I stood in the burned-out shell of our synagogue, and I was alone.

"And suddenly I realized what day it was—it was Shabbat Shirah, the Sabbath when we read the story of the crossing of the Red Sea. And the birds came, all the birds, as they had come every year to eat the children's crumbs and to sing with us! But there were no children, and there were no crumbs for the birds. The birds were starving in the cold of the winter. So I decided I must save them. I couldn't save the children, and I couldn't save the song, but perhaps I could save the birds. I picked up the birds and put them in these cages. I picked up as many as I could carry. And I have brought them here. Here there are Jewish children. Here there is Jewish song. Here there is Jewish life. Here there is a future for the birds and for Jewish children. So here the birds will live again."

The astonished officer stamped the rabbi's passport and said with reverence, "Welcome to Israel, Rabbi Elimelech son of

Shlomo of Chelm. Here you will find Jewish children. Here you will find Jewish people who sing. Here you and your birds will find life again. Welcome to Israel, Rabbi."

The most catastrophic moment in ancient Jewish history was the destruction of the Temple by the Romans. In modern times we have suffered a tragedy of equal devastation in the Holocaust. The greatest moment of redemption in ancient Jewish history was the Exodus. In modern times we have witnessed an event of equal wonder in the rebirth of Israel. The Talmud teaches, "The recipient of a miracle cannot perceive his miracle" (Talmud Niddah 31b). Only after some time will we fully appreciate what has happened to us in this generation. In the meantime, all we have are stories.

- What do you suppose it was like for the rabbi to return home only to discover that he was the only one to have survived?

- What do the birds in this story represent?

- Have you ever met a survivor of the concentration camps? How do you suppose survivors of the concentration camps found the courage to go on with life after the Holocaust?

The Flag of Israel

Most of us have grown up with the State of Israel. But there was a time very recently when Israel was only an idea and a dream. Israel had to be invented. And everything about it had to be considered—what form of government it would have, who its leaders would be, what language its inhabitants would speak. Even its flag needed to be created.

A hundred years ago there was no sovereign state called Israel. Jews lived all over the world—in Europe, America, the Middle East, Africa, Australia, and Asia—but they lived in countries that belonged to others. The idea that Jews could return to their homeland and have a country that belonged to them was the invention of a great thinker, Theodor Herzl. A Jewish country was Herzl's dream.

To make this dream come true, Herzl worked tirelessly. He wrote books, met with world leaders, and organized the Jewish community. His goal was to persuade the world to give the Jewish people a country in their ancient homeland. In August 1897 he held a great meeting of Jewish leaders to show them the way to create this new Jewish country. This meeting was the First Zionist Congress, and it was held in the city of Basel, in Switzerland.

A few hours before the meeting was to begin, Herzl realized that he had forgotten something important. If the Jewish people were to have a new country all their own, they needed a flag. Every country has a flag. But what would be the design of the flag of this new Jewish country? And where in the city of Basel could he find it?

With the meeting beginning and the room filling up with important leaders, Herzl had much to do. So he turned to his friend David Wolfsohn and asked him to find a flag for the new Jewish country. Wolfsohn ran up and down the boulevards and avenues of the city looking for something that could be used as a flag. He worried: What color should it be? What symbol should it have? And where was he going to find it in the few minutes he had before the meeting began?

Wolfsohn loved Herzl, and he loved Herzl's dream of a new Jewish country. He didn't want to fail in his mission or make a mistake, but he was running out of time. There was no flag to be found, and in the summertime heat he was growing very tired. He found a small synagogue on one of the streets of Basel, and he decided to stop there for a moment of rest.

As Wolfsohn was sitting in the synagogue, the rabbi came by to greet him and ask if he needed help. Wolfsohn explained his mission: The meeting of the First Zionist Congress was about to begin. It was his job to find a flag to represent the new Jewish country that the Zionists would create. But what kind of flag, and where to find it? Wolfsohn had run out of ideas.

The rabbi listened with sympathy. "I'm sorry," he said, "but I have no material for a flag here in the synagogue. All I have is this *tallis,* which we wear when we pray."

Wolfsohn's eyes grew wide with wonder. Of course. What better flag for the new Jewish country? For more than eighteen hundred years, Jews had wrapped themselves in a *tallit* and prayed, asking God to bring them home to their ancient land as a free people. They had gathered up the four fringes of the *tallit* and recited:

V'havi'eynu l'shalom m'arba kanfot ha'aretz.
Gather us in peace from the four corners of the earth.
V'tolee'chayn komumi'yut l'artz'eynu.
And bring us upright to our land.

What better flag for the new Jewish country?
Wolfsohn asked for a *tallis,* a white *tallis* with two blue stripes on either end. To transform the *tallis* into a flag, he removed the

tzitziot, the holy fringes. Then Wolfsohn took out his fountain pen, and between the blue stripes he carefully drew a six-pointed star, the Magein David, the legendary shield of King David.

Wolfsohn ran back to the meeting hall. Just before Herzl called the First Zionist Congress to order, Wolfsohn unfurled his new flag. The dignitaries and leaders of Jewish communities from all over the world stood and applauded the new flag.

Fifty-one years later, in 1948, the State of Israel was established. And Wolfsohn's flag was declared the flag of the State of Israel. A country whose flag is a *tallis* is the answer to all our prayers.

"As long as the heart of the Jew beats,
And as long as the eyes of the Jew look eastward,
Our two-thousand-year hope is not lost,
To be a free nation in Zion, in Jerusalem"
—*"Hatikvah,"* Israel's national anthem,
by Naftali Herz Imber

For nearly two thousand years, Jews waited and hoped and prayed to return to the land of their birth. Only a few years ago, in the middle of the twentieth century, were we to see this dream and this prayer come true. The wonder of Israel's rebirth should never be lost to us. It is one of the great miracles of the Jewish experience. But neither should we forget that this dream took the efforts and even the lives of so many to become a reality.

- How do you suppose it felt to be in the hall in Basel when Herzl opened that first Zionist meeting?

- Why is the State of Israel so important to the Jewish people? How is its flag a clue to this importance?

- What are some of the ways in which having our own Jewish country has changed the life of the Jewish people?

The Knapsack

*Part of growing up is discovering who we really are.
Part of growing wise is discovering what story is really
ours. Sometimes the process comes easily. We are who we
seem to be—someone's son or daughter, someone's partner and friend. We are defined by the work we do, the
communities we join, the things that interest us. But
sometimes our true identity comes as a great surprise.*

At the end of the nineteenth century, more than five million
Jews lived under the rule of the czar of Russia. The czar
hated the Jews. He decided to divide them into thirds: One third
he would convert, one third he would chase out of Russia, and
one third he would destroy. He issued orders to kidnap all Jewish
boys age eight and above and force them to serve in his army for
ten years. Thousands of Jewish boys were stolen from their families.
In the army of the czar, they forgot who they were and where they
came from.

Once an elderly Jewish couple in a tiny Russian village was
forced by the government to take in a soldier who was marching
with his troop through the countryside. The couple moved out of
their bedroom, and the young man, all gruffness and glares,
moved in, with his pack and rifle and bedroll. He lay on their bed,
ramrod straight, as if he were still standing at attention, his boots
still laced tightly on his feet, and stared at the ceiling in silence.
Every question, every invitation to engage in conversation, was
met with a grunted single-word answer, usually *nyet!* "No!"

It was Friday night. The couple prepared to sit down for
Shabbat dinner. The soldier took his place at the table. He glared

at them with contempt. Only now could they see just how young he was.

As the old woman kindled the Shabbat candles, covered her eyes, and recited a blessing, his eyes grew softer, and he stared with wonder. The words were strange to him. But the scene was familiar. In some way he recognized the rhythm and melody of her prayer. He listened as the old man chanted the Kiddush and Hamotzi. Once again the prayers were strange to him but somehow familiar. He knew none of the words, but the melody—he knew it from somewhere, from some time.

The soldier quickly devoured the hunk of challah placed before him, and, speaking for the first time, he asked for more. His voice was not that of a hardened soldier but that of a boy lost in the world.

His face was a picture of bewilderment. Something about this picture—the sight of the candles, the melody of the prayers, the taste of the challah—was familiar. It touched him in some mysterious way. But how? How could it be? He had never been here before, had never met these people, had never visited this village. How could it be familiar?

Suddenly the young man arose from his seat at the table and beckoned the old man to follow him, back into the bedroom. He pulled his heavy pack from the floor onto the bed and began to pull things out—clothes, equipment, ammunition—until finally, at the very bottom, he pulled out a small velvet bag tied with a drawstring.

"Can you tell me, perhaps, what this is?" he asked the old man, his eyes now gentle and imploring.

The old man took the bag in trembling fingers and loosened the string. Inside were a child's *tallis*, tiny *tefillin*, and a small book of Hebrew prayers. "Where did you get this?" he asked the soldier.

The soldier answered, "I have always had them. I don't remember when…"

The old man opened the prayer book, and he read the flyleaf, his eyes filling with tears: "To our son, Yossele, taken from us as a boy. Should you ever see your bar mitzvah, know that you are a Jew. Be proud. And know that wherever you are, your mama and papa always love you."

The old man closed the book, turned to the soldier, and embraced him. The young soldier tried to fight back the tears, but he was unsuccessful. His tears and the tears of the old man mingled as the old man whispered into his ear, "Welcome home, Yossele, welcome home."

"The soul of man is the lamp of God."
—Proverbs 20:27

Each of us carries a point of God's light. But most of us have forgotten about it. Our divine light lies hidden deep within the knapsack we carry through life, under our anxieties, our unfulfilled plans, our disappointments and failures. But it's there, waiting for us. And the deeper purpose of religious life is to allow us to discover and strengthen that spark of divine light within us.

- Of all the things the young soldier experienced in the old couple's home, which one do you suppose truly connected him with his memories of being Jewish?

- What do you think happened next? What do you think the old man told the boy?

- Was the old man Yossele's father, or was he welcoming Yossele back to the Jewish people?

Values Index

Value	Stories
Activism	Please Don't Eat That Sheep!; Splitting the Sea; The Maccabees' Sister; The Cursed Harvest; The Holy Thief
Ambition	The Sukkah of Rabbi Pinchas; Akiva and Rachel; The Rabbi and the Gladiator; Finding God
Charity	Heaven and Hell; The Holy Miser; Elijah's Gifts; Challahs in the Ark; The Magician
Collective responsibility	It's Not My Problem; Heaven and Hell; Day and Night; Please Don't Eat That Sheep!; Splitting the Sea; The Maccabees' Sister; The Cursed Harvest; The Storyteller; The Knapsack
Community	It's Not My Problem; Heaven and Hell; The Holy Miser; Day and Night; Challahs in the Ark; The Holy Thief; Capturing the Moon; The Sukkah of Rabbi Pinchas; Lifting the Torah; The Last Story of the Wise Men of Chelm; The Knapsack
Companionship	Paradise; Elijah's Gifts; Capturing the Moon; The Magician
Compassion	The Jester; Heaven and Hell; The Holy Miser; Elijah's Gifts; The Magician

Contentment	Paradise; Diamonds and Potatoes; Turning Your Shoes Around; Elijah's Gifts; Challahs in the Ark; Capturing the Moon; The Sukkah of Rabbi Pinchas; The Magic Ring; The Magician
Courage	It's Not My Problem; Elijah's Stick; The Maccabees' Sister; The Holy Thief; The Storyteller; The Rabbi and the Gladiator
Creativity	The True Artist; Please Don't Eat That Sheep!; The Diamond; The Flag of Israel
Dreaming	The Treasure; Diamonds and Potatoes; Elijah's Stick; The Magician
Education	Akiva and Rachel; The Rabbi and the Gladiator; Finding God
Fairness	The Tailor and the Prince; Please Don't Eat That Sheep!; The Holy Thief
Faith	Splitting the Sea; Challahs in the Ark; The Storyteller; The Magician
Family	Diamonds and Potatoes; The Tailor and the Prince; Challahs in the Ark; Akiva and Rachel; Finding God; The Knapsack
Friendship	The Tailor and the Prince; The Bird in the Tree; The Rabbi and the Gladiator
Heroism	Splitting the Sea; Elijah's Stick; The Maccabees' Sister; The Holy Thief
Home	The Treasure; Diamonds and Potatoes; Turning Your Shoes Around; Finding God; The Magician
Honesty	The True Artist; The Holy Thief
Humility	Diamonds and Potatoes; The Jester; The Holy Miser; Challahs in the Ark
Inner wealth	Paradise; Diamonds and Potatoes; The Magic Ring; The Magician

Special Occasion	Stories
First day of school	Akiva and Rachel; Finding God
Graduation	The True Artist; It's Not My Problem
Hanukkah	The Maccabees' Sister
Pesach	Elijah's Gifts; Splitting the Sea; Elijah's Stick; Lift Up Your Eyes and See; The Magician
Retirement	Paradise
Rosh Chodesh	Capturing the Moon
Rosh Hashana and Yom Kippur	The Holy Thief; The Storyteller; The Diamond; Hiding God's Image
Shabbat	Challahs in the Ark; Lifting the Torah
Simchat Torah	Lifting the Torah
Sukkot	The Sukkah of Rabbi Pinchas
Wedding anniversary	Paradise
Yom Ha'atzma'ut	The Flag of Israel
Yom Hashoah	The Last Story of the Wise Men of Chelm